BLESSINGS OF FIRE AND ICE

A Norse Witch Devotional

About The Author

Connla Freyjason prefers to think outside the box, even as he practices the Old Ways. Having spent the past twenty years as a Pagan, he is fulltrui (a dedicant) of Freyja, a practicing vitki, and also a digital artist and graphic designer. The "presiding spirit" currently "horsed" by Ollamh Michelle Iacona, he is also the primary author of the Iaconagraphy blog.

BLESSINGS OF FIRE AND ICE
A Norse Witch Devotional

Connla Freyjason

via Michelle Iacona

Iaconagraphy Press

Massachusetts

First published in 2018 by Iaconagraphy Press
Massachusetts
www.michelleiacona.com

FIRST EDITION

Author Photo: S. Hersey

Book Design: George Fitzgerald, Michelle Iacona, & Frances Keys

Cover Art & Illustration: Connla Freyjason

Interior Illustration: Connla Freyjason

ISBN 978-0692136034

facebook.com/Iaconagraphy

*For all those who wish to live daily with the
Gods;*

*For all the mavericks, blazing the trail of a
living faith, against all odds;*

&

For Suzanne, who helped me remember:

I'm a poet.

~Connla

I am the cat in the darkness,
I am the rose and the thorn,
I am the falcon on the wing,
And the whisper of air which lifts her up.
I am the artist and I am the art;
The maker, and the made.
I am the silence between the words
That gives the meaning to what's been said.
I am the Lover;
I am the Beloved.
I am what lies between.

~Connla Freyjason
For Freyja....

CONTENTS

Acknowledgments ix

Foreword xi

ACKNOWLEDGMENTS

People tend to think of writing as a lonely endeavor, but in truth, it is anything but. This book would have been impossible without a number of people, and I would like to thank them again, even though they are all likely very tired of hearing those two little words from me by now.

Michelle Iacona, because without you, I absolutely *would not* be here. You have given up more than any one human should ever have been asked to give up over the past twenty-four years of our relationship as Horse and Rider, and "thank you" is simply too small to encompass what you mean to me. You are so much more than "just a writer", and I hope this book finally proves that to the entire world.

Suzanne, my Beloved and my very best friend. You are my wife-of-the-heart, and that means far more than a piece of paper ever could. Your patience and your ability to love *because* not *despite* never cease to amaze me. I never could have believed in myself enough to write this book, or make art, or even simply *keep going*, if you hadn't believed in me first.

Jan Tjeerd, for becoming first and foremost a dear friend, and second, the greatest cheerleader a guy could ever want. Thank you for continually pushing me out onto limbs I never dared to dream of, and then graciously celebrating as I soar. Thank you, also, for becoming my absolute favorite "partner in crime and faith". Poetry runs through your very veins, my friend; one day, I will convince you of it!

Lawrence Hoffman, my heart-brother: your faith in me has never wavered, and your friendship is priceless.

Sharon, "Little Sister":   it's been a long road together, but worth every step of the trip. Thank you for teaching me endurance, especially on those days when I didn't think I had another ounce of strength left in me.

Linda, my mother-of-the-heart, thank you for adopting me. No matter how "weird" it has ever been, you have always been there for me, with kindness and wisdom, shaping my Wyrd for the better.

Alfred McCarthy, for helping me find my footing on this path, and reminding me always what it means to be not only a good witch and a good writer, but also a good man.

Ivy Mulligan, for recognizing me as a fellow maverick on this many-colored and winding road, and for fanning the flames of our shared Heidhrinn Hearts.

Kriselda Gray, for reminding me what the word "warrior" really means. You are one, my dear, every day!

My Ancestors of Flesh and Blood, for gifting me with an ever-open mind.

My Ancestors I have gained through Michelle: Mema, thank you for the gift of an ever-open heart, to go with my ever-open mind.

And most of all: Freyja.
Thank You for choosing me as one of Your representatives here in this mundane world, and thank You for giving me the courage to attempt to bring the shimmer of the Northern Lights into the lives of others. I hope I do not disappoint....

FOREWORD
BY JAN TJEERD

There are many in the Heathen community who are very quick to pronounce "you are doing it wrong!" when it comes to practices of a magical, modern, or "not found in the lore" nature. By their own ideal of "what Heathenry was then", those attitudes often fail to recognize or acknowledge a very important element: that of constant experiential reveal. In the very time period which many have selected as *the* point for all things Heathen or Asatru, the People were acting on the gnosis that was revealed to them at that time to create then-modern experiences--all without the "lore". What this form of dogmatic clinging to an imagined religious system has done for many is to strengthen their resolve to develop the relationships with those Beings in a way that is relevant to life in the 21st century.

Enter Connla Freyjason. Connla has accomplished much during his existence and has beaten the odds to continue to grow and share the passion he has for a vibrant and interactive relationship with Gods and Goddesses, supernatural Beings and spirits of nature (land and house vaettir). As an artist for many years and student of different paths of spirituality, he has met the Gods and Goddesses of the Northern European lands and is thriving in the experiences he is having with Them and eager to share that with others. These opportunities are translating to life lessons about spirituality by building upon the legacy of our ancestors and engaging with the diverse and wonderful, powers of the Nine Worlds.

Since the Gods did not cease to exist or go into a dormant state during the years of religious suppression by dominant monotheism, They continued to change and live even while most of humanity paid no attention to Them. With the revival of polytheistic acceptance in much of the Western world in the last hundred years or so (and more emphatically within the last fifty years), humans are once again reaching out to the Gods of various cultures that had long been relegated to fairy tales and superstition.

What we find in meeting Them again, is that while we have many of Their stories preserved in texts, translations and remnants of traditions, They have moved beyond those snapshots of who They were just as humanity has. We must get to know them as They are now and not continue holding Them to who *we think* They were then. This is not always easy for some, as they want a defined unchangeable source for the foundation of their practice. The thought of the Gods being changeable and expanding beyond the sagas and eddas preserved is often a frightening concept to accept.

In his book *Norse Witch: Reclaiming the Heidhrinn Heart*, Connla created a dialogue and sacred safe space in which those who feel the call of the Northern Gods, Goddesses and Beings could practice within a modern context as they are being led. His deep connection and personal relationships to those Beings builds upon a foundation of the lore, sagas, Old Norse language, and archaeological findings.

This foundation is a great starting point from which to learn how our ancestors may have practiced or reacted to the Gods and helps us to understand how They chose to express Themselves to the people of that time and in the places where our ancestors resided. But just as a person is not the same as they were described in a high school year book thirty years later, neither are the Gods exactly the same as They are described (or interpreted) in the extant copies of the lore today.

In his books, Connla sets out to reclaim the Heathen (or Heidhrinn) *heart*--that of connecting by *your own* experiences to Those of the Nine Worlds. While *Norse Witch* set the foundation and laid out some tools, *Blessings of Fire and Ice* provides ways to learn how to apply those tools to a thriving modern spiritual practice.

The poems within this work integrate lessons and experiences of our ancestors preserved in the eddas and sagas as well as modern experiences and interpretations. They include stories of the past, experiences of the present, and inspiration from the heart and soul.

In a world where many are expressing their desire to separate and exclude, this book waters the seeds of the beautiful blooms of diversity, unity, and inclusivity. Connla intends to set forth a number of works, each building upon and supporting the ideals presented and encouraging those to be expressed and shared with others. *Blessings of Fire and Ice* is the second in that series.

I invite you to join Connla and other Norse Witches in discovering your own journey of the Nine Worlds....

Jan Tjeerd
Host of *Gifts of the Wyrd*
California
May, 2018

BLESSINGS OF FIRE AND ICE

A Norse Witch Devotional

I've dreamed of flames nine nights now;
Nine nights, hung upon a pyre of spears,
Burning,
Like Gullveig.
Those flames,
The flames of condescension
        and derision,
Sparked by all those who would
        claim Heathen,
Without understanding or accepting
        what it is to be
Heidhrinn.
I've dreamed of flames nine nights now;
Nine nights, hung upon a pyre of spears,
Burning,
Like Gullveig.
Each time,
Thrice-burned,
Thrice-born,
To become Heidhr.
And now the smoke has cleared;
I see the path that lies before me
        with clarity,

As I could never see before.
I am Heidhrinn, not Heathen:
Bright and shining;
A prophesying witch,
My wand, enchanted;
For I am versed in magick,
And wherever I go, spirits are at play,
Including my own.
I bring healing to those in need of it,
And magick where once there was none.
I *am not* woman,
But I *am* witch.
I've dreamed of flames nine nights now;
Nine nights, hung upon a pyre of spears,
Like Gullveig.
And I burn
To ignite the flames of others,
Where once only ashes
        of the past held sway.

~Connla Freyjason

THE WHEEL OF FIRE AND ICE

When talking about any religion, one of the first things that usually comes up in conversation are that faith's holy days of observance: **holidays**. Christians have Christmas and Easter, of course; Jews celebrate Hanukkah and Passover; Muslims observe Ramadan. Meanwhile, Pagans and Wiccans have their Wheel of the Year, with Samhain, Yule, Imbolc, Beltane, Midsummer, Lughnassadh, and Mabon. So what about those following a Norse Path? Like so many other things in modern Heathenry, this is a widely varied and sometimes hotly contested subject. In fact, which holidays are observed often depends on whether one is a *devout* Historical Reconstrustionist or not, as well as to which Kindred or major organization one belongs. Some organizations and strict Reconstructionists base their observances around their understanding of the Old Icelandic Calendar (which even the people of Iceland no longer use), while others attempt to ally their "wheel of the year" with the more traditional Pagan one, as well as with mundane-world observances, such as Memorial Day (as with the Troth).

As followers of an Old Way living in a modern world, it becomes necessary to rely on historical resources as well as good, old-fashioned common sense when creating a calendar of potential observances for the practicing Norse Witch. Most practitioners of Heidhrinnry will either already belong to an established organization (such as the Troth), will be observing the High Days with another local Pagan group that is not necessarily Norse-based (in which case, they will be observing the traditional Pagan Wheel of the Year), or will be solitary. Neither profoundly overthinking the issue, by expecting people to adopt a dead calendar, nor wholesale adopting the presently accepted Pagan calendar, while completely ignoring the historical basis of our High Days, is terribly productive. In fact, both completely sap our holidays of their spiritual significance.

This book is organized according to the Wheel of the Year as I celebrate it as a Heidhrinn Norse Witch: a Wheel of Fire and Ice which begins and ends each year at Winternights (Mabon in other Pagan traditions). Like the traditional Pagan Wheel of the Year, we likewise find the Heidhrinn Wheel of the Year divided into a Dark Half and a Light Half: one of Ice, and one of Fire. Contrary to surface appearances, this is not based on any personal attempt to hammer a Norse-based tradition into some sort of "New Age framework", but instead on solid history. Worms runic calendar (depicted in the book *Fasti Danici*, published 1626) allegedly dates from 1328. Although the actual artifact has been lost to time, the drawings within that book depict a whale or porpoise bone, carved with runes representing *one half* of the year, beginning at the 13th or 14th of October, and ending on April 13th. We are told that the other half of the artifact contained the other half of the year, which supports an understanding of a "halved year" by our Norse Ancestors.

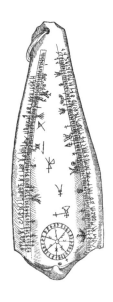

As with other practices covered within my *Norse Witch Series*, your "mileage may vary", as to which holidays you celebrate, and how. Because my non-solitary practice is with a non-Norse-based group (I am a General Member of the Temple of Witchcraft in Salem, New Hampshire), you will find that my construction and observance of the Heidhrinn Wheel of the Year has equal amounts in common with the typical Pagan Wheel, and with the Troth's calendar of observances. As much as possible, I have attempted to allow the historical record (particularly the archaeological record) to inspire these choices. Ultimately, all I can do is work from my own realm of experience, and hope that it touches some small part of *your* experiences. Many kind and wonderful people have made the request that I compose a devotional for the practicing Norse Witch, and I have tried my utmost, with the Gods' gracious help, to pour blessings into this book worthy of those requests.

This is, first and foremost, precisely that: a book of blessings. On a particularly grey day in April, I found myself faced with the sudden need to pick up the pieces, while my Publishing Editor fell apart. So I did what any good Norse Witch would do: I prayed, and then I pulled a rune. That rune was Ansuz (ᚠ):

> By your Hallowed Names,
> I charge this rune:
> Ansuz.
> Odin's Rune;
> God-Rune;
> Rune of blessings spoken.
> Sign of communication and inspiration;
> Of Wisdom and Truth.
> With your help, I advise against vanity,
> manipulation, and misunderstanding.
> I paint you the purple of the royal Aesir;
> I prove you through wise words, clear
> communication, inspired speech, and
> blessings bestowed.
> I pray you: *Bless.*
> I blot you with poetry and the blessing of others.
> I send you forth as inspiration, wisdom, and
> blessings for myself;
> Inspiration, wisdom, and blessings for those I hold
> dear.

Rather than basing this book on the typical "hook, book, look, took" method used by most Christian devotionals, the Gods made it very clear to me from the onset that this book was meant to be something different. They intended for it to be a ray of light in an otherwise dark world, and I solemnly pray that it will be.

A period of devotional activity may already be a part of your daily routine, and, if so, I hope this book becomes a part of that. If not, I suggest setting aside a few minutes each morning not only to spend a bit of time with this book, but also to light a candle or incense on your altar, and offer prayers to the Deity corresponding to that day of the week, as well as to your Fulltrui/Fulltrua. Don't worry if this book has arrived in your life at a time other than Winternights. I have attempted to design it so that the devotional blessings within may be picked up at whatever time of the year this book crosses your path. For those living in the Southern Hemisphere, I invite you to use your normal practice as your guide through this book.

One month and one day after having begun, I can honestly say that this book which you now hold in your hands has been precisely the blot-of-poetry which Ansuz invites. I pray it serves you likewise.

Shine on!
Connla Freyjason,
May 19, 2018

THE SEASON OF ICE

WINTERNIGHTS, ALFABLOT, YULE, DISABLOT, SIGRBLOT

WINTERNIGHTS
SEPTEMBER 21

Seeds sown in Spring,
Grown through Summer:
Peace and good seasons
In the Season of Fire.
Seeds sown in harrows:
Corpse to birth, and back again:
I remember my Ancestors
At the dawn of the Season of Ice.
Welcome Winter!
One last pour for Freyr:
To embers dying
To be born again
With seeds sown in Spring.

WINTERNIGHTS

SEPTEMBER 22

I blot at the rise of winter
For a good year to come:
Hail Holy Freyr!
Bright Freyr:
I plant this seed
At Winternights:
That I may (insert your goal here) in the coming
   year,
That it bring peace and good seasons in my life,
And in the lives of those whom I hold dear.
See this seed I've planted;
These things I have stored up:
These bright provisions put away,
For the winter that is soon to come.
As bird and bear,
As squirrel and mouse,
I prepare and am prepared;
I go inside, to move forward.
Hail Holy Freyr!
Bright Freyr:
I plant this seed
At Winternights.

WINTERNIGHTS

SEPTEMBER 23

Freyr,
er lengi hefir fulltrúi minn verið
og margar gjafar að mér þegið og vel launað,
nú gef eg þér...

Freyr,
Long have You been One in Whom I put my trust
And many good gifts I have accepted and (been)
  rewarded well,
Now I give this....

For all I have been given,
And all that You will give:

Thank You.

--Portions from *Viga-Glums Saga*, my own translation

WINTERNIGHTS

SEPTEMBER 24

By your Hallowed Names,
I charge this rune:
Raidho.
Hela's Rune;
Wagon-Rune;
Rune of travels and journeys.
Sign of relocation and evolution;
Of new horizons and the dance of life.
I carve you thus;
With your help, I advise against rigidity, injustice,
    and stagnation.
I paint you the black of long roadways;
I prove you by seeking new horizons and enjoying
    the journey of life.
I pray you: *Move me.*
I blot you with wight-walks and by feeding my skin-
    bag.
I send you forth as fair travels and bright horizons
    for myself;
Fair travels and bright horizons for those I hold
    dear.

WINTERNIGHTS

SEPTEMBER 25

Dwells in dales
The curious Dis,
From Yggdrasil's
Ash-tree gently fallen;
Alfa-clanned
Idunna-named,
Of Ivaldi's eldest
Youngest born.
Bring the apples;
Restore our youth!
Rejuvenating One,
Remind us to be light of heart,
Even as the days grow dark.

--Portions from *Hrafnagaldur Odins*, Stanza 6,
my own translation

WINTERNIGHTS

SEPTEMBER 26

Wandering the Great Wood,
By Orchard's hedge,
The Burden of Bragi's Arms,
Taken by flight:
Thjazi comes to steal the alf-maid;
Apple-Dis;
Rejuvenator.
And Loki begs a favor
Of Vanadis.
Hawk-flight to acorn;
Seed to stem;
Bring the apples back again!
Fire blaze and feathers fly;
Aesir reclaim what Thjazi would deny!
Promise from the oak does fall:
By leaf and twig,
The many-colored world, a skald,
Telling tales of flames a-blaze,
And Gods renewed
By Idunna and her orchard-fruit.

WINTERNIGHTS

SEPTEMBER 27

Wronged Skadi
Did not grieve,
But Her Wergild
Would receive.
With bow and ski,
Did make Her way
To Bifrost's shimmering light.
Above the World-Tree,
Arched by pyre,
Skadi spoke Her deserved desire:
"Make me laugh,
Then bride I'd be!"
No tears to shed,
But bold-faced She!
And Odin,
He gave this decree:
"By feet alone
Your suitor choose!"
In a line,
The Gods They came,
As Loki plied a goatish game.
Skadi laughed
As goat did tug
A groaning, aching
Trickster's bulge,
And from the feet of Gods at hand,
The best and brightest She did choose:
Njordr, not Baldur as was planned;
Merchant, sailor, peace-keeping man.
Thus did Summer come to Winter,
And Winter to the strand.

SEPTEMBER 28

By your Hallowed Names,
I charge this rune:
Laguz.
Njordr and Aegir's Rune;
Water-Rune;
Rune of flowing, healing, and organic growth.
Sign of imagination and the Otherworld;
Of dreams, mysteries, and the unknown.
I carve you thus;
With your help, I advise against confusion, poor
  judgment, apathy, fear, avoidance, and
  depression.
I paint you the blue and white of crashing waves;
I prove you each time I dream; each time I seek the
  Otherworld; each time I understand that
  there is more to this world than the
  mundane; each time I create something
  beautiful and new.
I pray you: *Heal, Cleanse, Create.*
I blot you with seawater and with shells and sand.
I send you forth as healing, creativity, and spiritual
  growth for myself;
Healing, creativity, and spiritual growth for those I
  hold dear.

SEPTEMBER 29

By your Hallowed Names,
I charge this rune:
Eihwaz.
Angrbodha's Rune;
Yew-Rune;
Rune of strength and reliability.
Sign of trustworthiness and dependability;
Of protection and the driving force to defend as
      well as acquire.
I carve you thus;
With your help, I advise against confusion,
      destruction, and weakness.
I paint you the green and white of the winter wood;
I prove you through endurance, honoring my word,
      and reaching my goals.
I pray you: *Trust*.
I blot you with honest words and honorable deeds.
I send you forth as strength, honor, defense, and
      drive for myself;
Strength, honor, defense, and drive for those I hold
      dear.

SEPTEMBER 30

Oathsworn and Honor-bound,
Let me be honest;
Let my words be kind,
Yet filled with Truth.
Let those words
Reflect the heart within:
A heart that is dedicated
To equity and fairness for all;
A heart that works toward
Putting things right,
When there is need for right to be done.
Long after the tongue
That speaks them is gone,
Let my words remain
As a legacy of
Honor,
Kindness,
Truth.
So mote it be.
Enda er, ok enda skal vera.

OCTOBER 1

East of Midgard,
Iron Wood old,
Where hag-shaped woman
Gives birth to wolves,
And dead men come alive
Again.
Reddened moon
And wind of storm,
Blackened sun
At winter's crossing
Again.
Come and come and come
Again
Again:
Shift my shape
And let me run
Where Iron-wolves howl
And troll-kin seethe.
Teach me to be
Shape-strong
And wise.
Blooden the seats of the Gods
With fresh offerings,
Yet let me be content
With bread and wine.

OCTOBER 2

Mother-of-Monsters;
Witch, dead-not-dead:
Angrbodha,
Wolf-Mother,
Hail Dark Chieftain
Of the Iron Wood!
Troll-woman:
Teach me balance
Of light and dark;
Of masculine and feminine;
Of mind and heart.
As days shorten
And winter comes,
Teach me to run
With the wolves,
Hair streaming behind;
Magick afoot.

OCTOBER 3

Bound-One,
I weep with you:
Not because you are bound
Unjustly--
For what was done,
Needed to be done--
But because I have been
Likewise bound
By necessity,
And I understand that pain.
We bind parts of ourselves:
The dark parts,
And the angry;
The broken,
And the scorned.
We bind and
Bind back again;
We hide,
And are hidden,
From those who find
Our personal Truth
Dangerous,
As they found yours.
Hail, Fenrir,
Mighty Wolf!
I weep with you,
Bound-One,
For I understand
Too well
Your tears.

OCTOBER 4

Bite the tail:
Infinity.
Space between spaces;
Time between times.
I stand at the center,
And I hold.
Bite the tail:
Affinity.
Like begets like:
Kingship, kinship,
Blood and bone.
Bite the tail;
Sovereignty.
Space between spaces;
I stand enthroned.

OCTOBER 5

STALLI BLESSING

(Top shelf or primary work surface)
In the names of the Aesir,
And in the names of the Vanir,
And even in the names of the Rokkr,
I call a blessing on this space,
That it be a place beyond places,
Standing in a time beyond time.

(Second shelf, secondary work surface, or base)
In the names of the Aesir,
And in the names of the Vanir,
And even in the names of the Rokkr,
I call a blessing on this space:
Odin, gift me Wisdom as I work here;
Tyr, gift me Honor and Justice;
Thor, grant this space both Simplicity and Power.

(Left side)
In the names of the Aesir,
And in the names of the Vanir,
And even in the names of the Rokkr,
I call a blessing on this space:
Freyr, grant that my work here bear fruit;
Freyja, help me stand between and see;
Njordr, bring peace to my heart when here I stand.

(Right side)
In the names of the Aesir,
And in the names of the Vanir,
And even in the names of the Rokkr,
I call a blessing on this space:
Loki, help me work here with Humility;

Sigyn, gift me with Compassionate Will;
Angrbodha, great Chieftain of the Iron Wood,
Teach me the Strength of my Duality,
As I work here in this place beyond places,
Standing in a time beyond time.
(Hallow Sign)

OCTOBER 6

Hail to the Rokkr!
And hail,
Even to the Rokkr!
Twilight Gods,
Of Liminality
And the Fringe:
Help me understand
Worlds within worlds
And worlds
Inside myself.
Distaff Gods,
Of Time
And of Wyrd:
Show me the way
To manifest;
To weave
Present into past,
Past into present,
And both
Into future.
Gods of Jerkin,
Cloak, and Dark:
Teach me
Compassionate endurance;
Protect and
Bind away
What would bring
Me to harm.
Comfort and console;
Listen and understand.
Hail to the Rokkr!
And hail, even to the Rokkr!

OCTOBER 7

Stand me at the gates
Where dwell behind
Trolldomr:
Troll-kunnar,
Wolf-wives,
Wolf-mothers.
Stand me at the gates
By the Ifing's roar,
And let me learn
To be elemental:
Like fire,
Warm, inviting;
Burned and biting.
Like earth,
Strong and cunning;
Verdant with growth
Overrunning.
Like ice,
Cold, enduring;
Shaping, flowing,
And maturing.
Stand me at the gates,
Iron Wood-encircling,
That I may be
Shape-strong,
Mind-strong,
Magick;
Bright.

OCTOBER 8

Pour the wine
To feed the ve;
At Menglodh's Gate,
Open the way:
She Who Is Pleased,
Be pleased.
Pour the wine
And kneel to pray;
At Menglodh's Gate,
Open the way:
By ecstasy,
Be seized
And seethe,
Riding the High Seat
Help me be
Transported:
To Otherworlds
Fare me forth,
And station me
At farther shores.
Pour the wine
To feed the ve;
At Menglodh's Gate,
Open the way!

OCTOBER 9

Nine nights hung
Upon the pyre:
Thrice-burned,
Thrice-born
Gullveig.
Prophesying witch;
Enchantress.
Bright Lady
Of Western skies
And golden fields,
Flame-worn
And kindled:
Hang me thus,
That I may burn.
Thrice-burned,
Thrice-born,
Bright-shining:
Make of me a
Prophesying witch;
Enchanted.

October 10

Fear not for
The dying of the
Light,
For the brightest
Burns within.
I light a candle
For the dying days,
Winter-dark;
Foreboding.
For in the flame
Tomorrows dance,
And I grow warm
In that knowing.
Bleed the wax
And burn the fire,
Flame inside rise
Ever higher.
I am Heidhr,
And She is me:
Bright-shining
Heidhrinn
Witch, I be!
Thrice-fold shadows
Cannot quell
The magick
That within me dwells,
Nor darkness
Shade the shimmering light
That within my heart
Burns blazing bright.

OCTOBER 11

Hospitality for the stranger,
And hygge for the home;
Blankets for the cold ones,
And food for the gnomes.
Nisse within my kitchen,
And tomten by my stair;
Stir the pot three times for luck,
And rest the spoon just there.
Pour a cup of something warm,
And curl up with a book;
Bless the husvaettir of here,
In every door and nook.

OCTOBER 12

Bless this broom.
Broom,
Bless this room.
Dust and flotsam
Carry away
Any careworn thoughts,
Into dustpan
And out the door
With worry and the lot.
Frigga,
Shake Your keys
And claim
This household
As Your own.
Bless the lintels
Of my doorway,
And make this house
A home.

OCTOBER 13

All hail:
The mothers,
And the sisters;
The daughters,
And the wives;
The women
Who raised us,
And the women
We raise up.
Lift them up,
And celebrate
The Disir of today:
The ones who are
What will be,
As well as ones
That were.
All hail:
The mothers,
And the sisters;
The daughters,
And the wives.
All hail,
The modern Dis!
Arise! Arise!

OCTOBER 14

Oh my Lady;
Keeper of the Keys!
Frigga teach me
To be the gentle parent;
The loving spouse;
The proud caretaker
Of this humble house.
Let there be warmth
And candleglow;
Let no guest
From my doorway go
Without a token
Of the hospitality
That is both mine
And Yours.
Blessed be.

OCTOBER 15

Hail, Hela!
Corpse-Mother,
Wolf-Sister,
Pale-Rider of Helhest;
Peace-Bringer;
Kiss away our
Sorrow,
And comfort us
In our grief.
Remind us to fall in love with life,
That we may live it well
In the forever Of Death.
Protect the Horse
And the Rider,
When the Dead
Come forth
To speak,
And remind us
Of our Ancestors
In those moments
When we are weak.

OCTOBER 16

Gossamer bridle,
Shoe and
Stone:
I beg your presence
In my humble home.
Helhest,
Journey-Horse;
Three-Hoofed Runner:
Carry me not into death,
But through the Nine,
And back again.
Gossamer bridle,
Shoe and
Stone:
I beg your presence
In my humble home.
Helhest,
Journey-Horse;
Three-Hoofed Runner:
Teach me the boundaries
Of that which cannot be owned;
Of how to be wild--
Undomesticated--
Yet still maintain self-control.
Gossamer bridle,
Shoe and
Stone:
I beg your presence
In my humble home.

OCTOBER 17

I see
Outside
Myself
The fore-runner,
Harbinger,
Change-bringer,
Catalyst,
Wyrd-keeper:
Fylgja.
Me-not-me;
Soul's fourth face,
Yet somehow,
Not.
Protect and warn;
Lead and guide.
Show me
Those things
Which others might
Hide.

OCTOBER 18

Shape-strong,
I bend my shape.
Mold and meld;
Break and be mended.
Furred or fanged,
Feathered or hoofed,
Fylgja-not-fylgja;
Self-not-self.
Shape-strong;
Cunning;
Wise.
Folding inwards;
Reaching out:
In astral form,
I move about.
Perhaps on padfoot;
Mayhap on wing,
I fare me forth
To worlds all nine,
And then I sink
Back to self-that's-mine.

OCTOBER 19

Greed and Hunger,
Sitting side by side
At the feet of their Master:
Fylgja and Hamr;
"Follower" and "Shape":
One to shape the future,
The other to shape our skin.
Geri and Freki,
Odin's wolves:
Shaman-teachers,
Two.
Run alongside me,
Ravenous:
Devouring all those things
Which bring me to
Doubt,
Worry,
Hate.

OCTOBER 20

Oh!
That you should fly!
Thought-on-the-wing;
That fleeting essence
Of what makes me, me;
Of what makes you, you.
Memory takes flight:
Hamingja,
As hard-won and fleeting
As fame.
Huginn and Muninn,
Odin's birds:
Black-winged
Ravens,
Reflecting
All-Father's Soul.

OCTOBER 21

In Time outside of time
I stand,
Horn and dagger,
Cup-in-hand;
Blot I pour
To Gods-of-mine,
Blood replaced
By juice or wine.
I raise a toast
To those held dearest,
And feel Their touch
As they come nearer.
Ages erase themselves
In the closing of an eye,
And I am bound back,
And back, and
Back again,
To Ancestors
Of Blood and Bone,
And Ancestors
Of Path-Not-Kin.

OCTOBER 22

Hour to hour,
Day to day,
Week to week:
We ponder the order of time.
The more we ponder,
The more of it slips away.
Week to week,
Day to day,
Hour to hour.
Mundilfari:
Time-Voyager,
Sun-Father,
Moon-Father,
Wise.
Trace the passage;
Set the course.
Let my moments not be wasted
In worry for the past,
Nor my hours spent
In vain attempts
To mold a future yet uncast.

OCTOBER 23

Hail, Mani! Moon-face!
Bright Charioteer,
Teach our hearts compassion,
As your heart is compassionate.
Remind us that we are all
Fellow travelers in this Middle-Earth.
Help us not to judge
By the surface of things,
But instead raise for us
A mirror:
A shadowed glass,
In which we may first
Envision
How others might
Likewise judge us.
Help us to be
Empathizers:
Ones who walk a moment
In the shoes of another,
And are better,
In the end,
For having done.

OCTOBER 24

Hail Nott!
Praise to She
Who brings
The Rest-Time,
And to She
Who births
The Day!
Free-fly
Hrimfaxi's mane,
And kiss the ground
With dew!
Grandmother of Thor,
I raise a cup for you,
And pour out
My gratitude
For the comforts
Of the Night:
For dreams sweet,
And dreams wise.
The solace of slumber;
The closing of eyes.
Peaceful nights
In every season;
Twinkle of starlight
At Day's completion.

OCTOBER 25

Farewell
Summer-bright!
Sun-faced Sunna,
Sweet good night!
Winter,
Come gently;
Ease over the land,
Like skin
Over bone.
Softly embrace us,
Chilly fingers
Caressing
Eaves and doorways.
Leave us not
Wanting,
As we enter this
Long good-night.
Cradle the buds
That will be new
Come Spring;
Ease the journeys
Of the birds on wing
To warmer shores.
May squirrel and bear
Have enough for
Their sleep,
And likewise my loved ones
Throughout Winter's Deep.

OCTOBER 26

Sunwise
May I fare-forth:
Into the West
Let me go,
For one last time,
And one first.
Carry me
To Vanaheim;
Tarry me
In golden fields
Full of horses,
And on distant shores
Where seabirds
Raise their voices.
Cradle me
At Folkvangr and
Draw for me
A draught in
Sessrumnir;
Yet,
Let me pass through:
To Golden Wood,
And orchard fair;
But for a moment,
Let me tarry there.
Then shall I pass
On and through,
Again to the East,
And Midgard true.
Carry me, carry me,
Fare me forth:
Sunwise.

OCTOBER 27

By your Hallowed Names,
I charge this rune:
Sowilo.
Sunna's Rune;
Sun-Rune;
Rune of success and honor.
Sign of the life force and positive change;
Of victory, health, wholeness, and the cleansing
    fire.
I carve you thus;
With your help, I advise against destruction, vanity,
    and wrath.
I paint you the yellow of the rising sun;
I prove you each time I find the power within me to
    make positive changes in my life.
I pray you: *Shine*.
I blot you with fire and honey; with time spent
    basking in the glow of the sun.
I send you forth as victory, health, and wholeness
    for myself;
Victory, health, and wholeness for those I hold
    dear.

OCTOBER 28

By your Hallowed Names,
I charge this rune:
Wunjo.
Vanir-Rune;
Joy-Rune;
Rune of comfort and pleasure.
Sign of prosperity and harmony;
Of fellowship and reward.
I carve you thus;
With your help, I advise against sorrow and
    alienation, strife and rage.
I paint you a peaceful blue;
I prove you through being happy, enjoying the
    pleasures of life, and living in harmony with
    others.
I pray you: *Gratitude*.
I blot you with joyous dancing and with laughter
    and song.
I send you forth as joy and prosperity for myself;
Joy and prosperity for those I hold dear.

OCTOBER 29

Hail Alfar!
Blessings and Honor
To You and Your kin,
And to any of my own kin
Who have come to serve You.
Blessings and Honor
To the Alfar:
To those who once walked beside us,
As our Ancestors and kin,
And to those who never did,
But are among us, just the same.
Peace and good seasons to you,
And may there ever be frith between us,
And between me and mine,
And those who have come before and who will
　　come after.
For all that you have done for us,
And for all that you will do;
For all that you have meant to us,
And for all that you will mean:
Peace and good seasons;
Love, gratitude, and honor.
Blessed be!

ALFABLOT

OCTOBER 30

Hail Holy Freyr!
Lord of the Mound,
Light the path for us
'Neath harrow
And hill;
Whisper words from us
To our beloved ones
In the hereafter,
Be they ever-living
In Hela's sweet embrace,
Or riding forth
From Folkvangr.
Whether sailing
On the Summer-Sea
Above the Halls of Aegir,
Or become
Winged-wise
Atop the Winding Stair,
Take them love from us,
Respect and honor,
Til we meet
Again.

ALFABLOT

OCTOBER 31

By your Hallowed Names,
I charge this rune:
Othala.
Jord's Rune;
Ancestor-Rune;
Rune of inheritance.
Sign of property and possessions; of spiritual
 heritage;
Of that which is truly most important to us.
I carve you thus;
With your help, I advise against a lack of order,
 totalitarianism, slavery, and that which would
 lead to an ill Wyrd.
I paint you the brown of cherished gravesides and
 good earth;
I prove you each time I embark on spiritual
 journeys; each time I honor my Ancestors and
 Hamingja.
I pray you: *Remember*.
I blot you each time I honor my Ancestors; with
 absinthe and wormwood.
I send you forth as security, increase, and
 abundance for myself;
Security, increase, and abundance for those I hold
 dear.

ALFABLOT

NOVEMBER 1

Beside the Great Tree,
See me stand,
Heart full of honor;
Cup in hand:
I raise the chalice
To the Lost Ones Found,
All ye Alfar,
Gather 'round.
Blot I pour
To Men of Kin:
All those Fathers
Gone before me.
Blood and bone,
You wove my skin;
Known and unknown,
I am your living story.
Blot I pour
To those of Path:
All those Vitki
Who paved this many-colored road.
Staff and rune,
You wove my skill;
First sung the tunes
I galdr still.
Blot I pour
To the Born-Not-Born:
All you Bright Ones
Of Wing and Morn.
Guide me to the Winding Stair,
And upwards,
Into Alfheim fair.

NOVEMBER 2

All you Dark Ones
Of leaf and twig;
Of dusky skin,
And mystery deep:
Hear me,
Dokkalfar!
I call for Magick;
Call for Sight;
Call for Defense,
In the dead of night.
Good things I bring;
Offerings fair.
For the Dark Elves,
Humble prayer:
Be of aid,
And harm me not;
Be assuaged,
And ne'er forgot.
Blessings
Of milk and honey
I give to Thee:
For the Underneath;
The Dark Company.

November 3

Dvergatal
I chant:
Motsognir,
Anarr,
Thror,
Vitr.
Suck the weariness
From my bones
And replace it
With hope;
Increase my
Wisdom.
Fundinn,
Fili,
Hannarr,
Nyr:
Find
Will;
Teach skill.
Make me new.

NOVEMBER 4

Nordhri:
I turn
To face
A many-colored sky.
Asgard-home,
Realm of Aesir:
Power of Ansuz
Bless this space.
Austri:
I turn
To face
The rising sun.
Jotunheim,
Realm of Wolves:
Power of Eihwaz
Guard this space.
Sudhri:
I turn
To face
The Dark space of the South.
Helheim,
Realm of Gentle Death:
Power of Raidho
Rejuvenate this space.
Vestri:
I turn
To face
The setting sun.
Vanaheim,
Realm of Vanir:
Power of Kenaz
Manifest and seal this sacred space.

November 5

Crafters,
Forgers,
Makers-Bright!
All ye Earthy Wights:
Dwarves,
Long-bearded,
Strong of hand;
Quick of thought,
And skilled with brand,
'Round me gather,
Help my cause.
Accept gift for gift,
And song for song;
Offerings given,
Poured and sung;
With gold and gems
Let halls be hung.
Crafters,
Forgers,
Makers-Bright!
Be friend,
And enter in!

NOVEMBER 6

By cavern deep
And chasm wide,
Fare me forth to
Svartalfheim:
Light the forges!
Hamr-find:
Edge of cliff;
Dvergheim.
Dokkalfar dance;
Hammer sing!
Sharp of stone
And heat of steam;
Radiant shine
Of gemstone's gleam:
Gift for gift
Craft for craft
Art for art
Thus art to have!

NOVEMBER 7

Amber:
Time-stone,
Tears of Freyja,
Stone of Time-Delayed;
Held captive.
Four there were
Who smithed it:
Brisingamen.
Dvalinn, The Delayer,
Understood
The soul of amber.
Alfrik, High Elf,
Knew The Lady's place
As Sister of Freyr.
Berling, Merchant-ship,
Knew The Lady's place
As Daughter of Njordr.
Grer,The Groer,
Knew the ways
Of crop and wound.
Through love
'Twas made:
Flame-torc;
Amber-necklace.
Passion fired that forge;
Fuels me now:
I shall not be delayed.
I take my place
Beside the Goddess.
Righteously, I ply my trade,
To heal the souls of Men,
And this Middle-Earth.

NOVEMBER 8

Don the necklace
And stand before
The Stalli,
New-blessed;
Bright.
I call The Lady
One last time
On this
November's night:
Hail to you,
Sweet Vanadis;
Hail to you,
Sweet-Fair!
The leaves are trailing
In the street,
And cold seeps everywhere.
Remind me
As the winter creeps
Of seeds sleeping
Beneath the earth,
And make of me
Such a seed,
Ripe for fresh rebirth.
Help me take this
Time inside
To rebuild my
Self-esteem,
And make of me
When Spring returns
A proud and beautiful being.

NOVEMBER 9

Gefn:
Sweet Giver;
Oh!
Sweet Sister,
Freyja!
Matronus Alagabius:
All-Giving-Mother,
Prepare me
For the gifts
I am to receive,
Whatever
Gifts they be.
Help me realize:
I *am* worthy.
I *am* deserving.
For there is a
Part of You
That lives still now
In me.

NOVEMBER 10

"Outdoor shrine he made me fenced and laden
  with stones,
Now coarse rubble that to glass has turned;
Reddened he [this altar] newly (with) ox blood;
Ever believed Ottar in goddesses!"
Let me be as Ottar was:
Devout;
Ever reddening
Hogr and ve
With offerings
To You,
Holy Freyja!
Blot let me pour
Of fine wine
And juice,
For You no longer crave
The blood of beings.
Instead,
Heart's-blood:
Those indivisible,
Ineffable
Pieces of a
(Wo)Man's soul.
Let me be that
For You;
To You.
Let me be as Ottar was:
Devout.

--Portions from *Hyndluljóð* , my own translation

November 11

Gerdh to guard
Our home,
Our life;
We praise You,
Gentle Etin-Wife!
Teach our hearts
To love
Because, not despite;
Our eyes
To see
The spark
Of hope,
Even in the darkest
Night.

NOVEMBER 12

Hidden Mother beneath the waves,
We see You now and make You known:

Nehalennia, Hail!
Hail, Lady of Ships!

In ancient times,
You steered the ships;
Guide us now through air, land, and seas....

Nehalennia, Hail!
Hail, the Bounty-Bearer!

Bountiful One,
Bless our deeds....

Nehalennia, Hail!
Hail, Fair Navigator!

Nehalennia,
We thank and honor You.

Nehalennia, Hail!
Hail, Hidden Mother!

--Italicized portions by Jan Tjeerd,
Gifts of the Wyrd

November 13

I call to Holda,
Kind and Gracious,
Faithful and True;
Queen of Heaven,
Hear my call to You:
Grandmother Winter,
Fluff Your feather-bed;
Let snow fall gently
On the good and the wise.
Let no ice tear and bite
Those who well-respect You.
Lead the Rade of the Disir
To doorway and to hearth,
To bless this house
And those within
With good seasons and peaceful hearts.
Lady of the Crossroads,
Help us to make good choices;
Remind us of the many sides
Of our own selves.
And should the honor come to me,
To join Your nighttime ride,
Let me put foot to stirrup
And ebon-wing to sky!

--With assistance from Frances Keys

NOVEMBER 14

Hail Sif!
Golden-haired
Frithful Mother,
Teach us to honor
Each other,
For that is the
Greatest bounty in life.
Help us pour out
Our blessings,
Even on those
Who have shown us
Short shrift,
And to keep the peace
In the darkest of times
Via the offering
Of frith.
As You did with Loki,
Let us do likewise:
"Hail the man you [are] now,
And take this foaming cup
Full of old honey-mead,
Rather you have one [and]
Leave with Gods' sons,
Unblemished."

--Portion from the *Lokasennna*, translation mine.

November 15

Hail Thrudh,
Thor's-Daughter!
Strength:
As mountains are strong;
As rock as it aches against water.
Steadfast;
Teach me to be likewise.
I will not crack.
I will not break.
I may change my shape,
But it will not be quickly,
Nor on a whim.
Strength:
As mountains are strong;
As rock as it aches against water.

November 16

Fulla:
Secret-Keeper,
Bountiful Maid,
Hail!
Bone to bone,
Blood to blood:
Help glue me
Back together,
When my life lays
In tatters upon the floor.
Show me
Ashen-boxed secrets of
Female Mysteries:
That I am
Householder;
Keeper of the Keys of the
Sovereign State of Me.
Wrap my head
In golden circlets;
Remind me
I am both Queen and King.
Bless my shoes
To walk my own path
With humility and justice,
And to walk a mile
In empathy
When needs be
For those less fortunate.

November 17

I ask Gna:
What there flies,
What there passes
Or glides in the sky?
Gna answers:
"I do not fly,
Though I move
And glide in the sky
On Hofvarpnir."
Hoof-Thrower,
Carry Her fair
Cross sea and sky.
Bright Messenger
Of Frigga,
Help me understand.
Keep my words
True and clear.
Open my lines of communication:
'Twixt Thee and me;
Mine and Thine;
Above, Below, and Elsewise.

--Portions from *Gylfaginning* 35, translation mine

NOVEMBER 18

Hail, Lofn!
Gentle and good,
Given leave by
All-Father
To govern
Human Intercourse:
Female and male;
That what was forbidden
Be so no more.
Lofn,
Give us leave to love
Whomever our heart
Decides,
And let not
Society deride
That which the Gods
Have blessed.

November 19

Syn
Gift me
With the
Power
Of the
Resounding "No".
Empower me
To understand
My ability to
Guard
My own gates.
Make of me a
Setter of boundaries;
An upholder
Of Justice,
Both my own and,
Where necessary,
For others.
A denial is made
When one says
"No";
Help me ever
To keep it so.

NOVEMBER 20

Wise and inquisitive
Vor,
Hark and Hail!
None may best You,
Nor conceal from You:
That person becomes thus aware
Of their worth as wise.
Teach me likewise to find
The wisdom within myself;
To look deep and divine
The Truth of me.
Unhide my own heart;
Lay it bare before my eyes,
That I may see what lies within.

--Portions from *Gylfaginning* 35, translation mine

November 21

Var,
Oath-Listener,
Agreement-Keeper:
It is promised to those who speak vows,
She avenges them, when broken.
Keep me to my word.
Bind me,
As does Tyr;
As does Forseti.
Bind me back,
And back again
To Truth.
Bind me forward,
And forward still,
Toward keeping It.
Mark my words,
As my words mark me.
Hear my oaths;
Seal my agreements.
May they be wisely wrought;
Well and wisely upheld.

--Portions from *Gylfaginning* 35, translation mine

NOVEMBER 22

Snotra Wise,
Stately of Manner;
Teach me
Temperance:
That all things
Are best
In moderation,
Including moderation.
Show me where
The balance lies,
That I may also
Be counted wise.
Gift me with sobriety
When I am at a loss,
And with joy and pride
When worthy for a cause.

November 23

Gefjun,
Giving One:
She who serves the young,
And is served in return
When Young Ones pass over
Into Worlds-Beyond,
Help, Hark, and Hear me:
Keep me young-of-heart,
And young-of-mind;
Teach me never to deride
Those who are thusly pure.
Let me not pass judgment
Upon the innocent,
Nor curb the youthful dreams
Of those with good intent.
Protect, we pray,
The teenager,
Faced with growing up too soon,
And likewise the
Parent/Teacher/Friend
Who provides their board and room.
Gift us strength
When we are challenged:
Boundaries broken;
Innocence curtailed.
Cradle us with warm words spoken
When we are thus assailed;
Remind us that it is
in our very vulnerability
That our truest strength prevails.

NOVEMBER 24

Raise the golden cup
And drink with me
Where strand meets sea
At Sokkvabekkr:
Saga,
Hail and well met!
Tales unravel
Where paradox
Meets poetry;
Cups emptied,
And stories told.
There, the wife,
Yet there, the sister;
Here, the byname
Of Frigga-Fair.
What?
Yet Freyja?
Distaff keeps the rhythm
For the telling.
I would yet no more,
And what?

NOVEMBER 25

Warden of the loving mind,
Sjofn, hear my call:
Turn hearts towards affection,
Where once was none at all.
Not the drive of passion,
Nor the burning of romance,
But the tender fashion
Of parent to child;
Of caregiver to the cared for,
Or the cared for to the giver.
Sjofn, I pray you:
Compassion to deliver.
Open hearts and open minds;
Set the course for love divine.
The kind that Gods share
With Their children,
And those children
With their Gods:
Love "because"--
Not "despite"--
To set this world to right.

NOVEMBER 26

Hlin to guard;
Hlin to guide:
This household,
This family;
These loved ones.
Grant solace
In our time of need;
Be the kind shoulder
On which to lean.
Shield-maiden of Frigga,
This blot I pour
To quench You
At Your post;
For Your comforts
Of the grieving,
I gladly raise this toast.
Hlin to guard;
Hlin to guide:
This household,
This family;
These loved ones.
Keep them safe
Both home and away,
And bring them back
Without obstructions.

NOVEMBER 27

Mercy, mercy be
Upon the sick
Or dying;
Great physician,
Valkyrie;
Menglodh's fair attendant:
Eir I honor,
Eir I call;
Eir I welcome to this hall.
Blot I pour
And herbs I reek:
Healing mercy yet I seek.
Worry, worry flee
Away from bedside
Harried be;
Replaced with gentle hand
And soothing touch.
Mercy, mercy be....

November 28

This season
That births
The Season;
This sweet series of
Mother-Nights:
Be blessed.
May I be blessed,
And mine be blessed,
And this home
With cheer be dressed
For the coming Yule.
Asynjur and Fair Disir,
We welcome You
To enter here,
And pass the time
By hearth and broom
With our family.
In this season
That births
The Season;
This sweet series of
Mother-Nights,
We offer up our blessings,
That we may be
Likewise blessed.
Gift for gift we give
And are given,
In this season
That births
The Season.

November 29

Raise the World Tree,
Evergreen,
To be the center of our home.
Deck it out with bright red thread;
Make it softly glow.
As the fir tree grew,
Where once stood
Thor's Great Oak,
Now again raise up
Our dreams
Of a Yule Season
Bright with hope.
The sun is long since sundered;
Winter is at hand.
Yet warmth surrounds
Each glad heart,
As the Yule tree once more stands.
Pass the warm mulled cider;
Raise a glass to Gods and Men,
For time has come
To celebrate:
The Wild Hunt rides again!
And in the quiet of the night
As the lights grow dim,
Let us offer up our solemn prayers
To Thor, Baldur, and Odin.
With gratitude,
Our hearts be filled;
With hope for the coming year:
Peace and good seasons to those we love,
And on Earth, joy and good cheer.

NOVEMBER 30

A cooking song
For hearth and home,
I raise my voice
In recognition
Of the spirits--
Tomte, Nisse, and Gnome--
Now dwelling in my kitchen!
Hail to the Husvaettir!
Hail and hail again!
Thank you for the peace you bring;
The bright warmth
And the hygge!
Thank you for the tasty things
That bubble,
Stew and brew here!
A cooking song
I gladly sing;
A blot of song,
I offer:
Hail and hail again!
Hail to the Husvaettir!

December 1

A friend shall prove himself a friend
And repay gift with gift;
Let me ever be
That type of friend.
Laughter with laughing
Takes hold of a house;
Let there be laughter
In my home
Without end.
Kindle the fire,
And warm the hearth;
Let ice blow outside,
Yet not in our hearts.
Fill up this home
With laughter and mirth;
When ordering our lives,
Let kindness come first.

--Portions from *Havamal* 42, translation mine.

DECEMBER 2

Cold silhouette of tree
Reaches black fingers
Towards a fading sun;
The nights grow longer still.
I shiver as I pour:
Blessed be to you,
Spirits of land and place;
Precious Landvaettir.
Teeth chatter
As I lay bread
At base of tree:
Blessed be to you,
Spirits of land and place;
Precious Landvaettir.
Bless the birds
That will soon dine,
Crumb by crumb
And seed by seed;
Bless the pebbles
'Neath my feet
As they absorb
Their juicy drink.
Bless the clouds
That bring the snow,
And the trees
That bear its weight.
Blessed be to you;
Blessed be me.

DECEMBER 3

Wind blow
Sky darken
Ullr hear;
Skadi harken:
Praise to the Gods
Of the Hunt!
Raise the glass
And join the chorus
Of storm-whipped
Icy trees:
Praise to the Gods
Of the Hunt!
Blot-dyed snow,
Red at my feet;
I watch it grow
Ever-deep:
Praise to the Gods
Of the Hunt!
Wind blow
Sky darken
Ullr hear;
Skadi harken:
Praise to the Gods
Of the Hunt!

December 4

By your Hallowed Names,
I charge this rune:
Jera.
Gerdha's Rune;
Harvest-Rune;
Rune of reaped rewards and fruitful seasons.
Sign of peace and happiness; of cycles and of
    change;
Of hopes, expectations, and successes earned.
I carve you thus;
With your help, I advise against bad timing,
    conflict, and reversals of fortune.
I paint you the brown of fertile earth;
I prove you each time I hope and dream; each time
    I accept and understand the cycles of life in the
    Universe; each time I work hard to manifest the
    things I dream.
I pray you: *Bring*.
I blot you by planting seeds and growing things.
I send you forth as peace and good seasons for
    myself;
Peace and good seasons for those I hold dear.

DECEMBER 5

Hunter and hunted,
Predator and prey,
Blood to blood,
Bone to bone,
Skin to hide,
And hide to skin,
I give you and am given;
I take you and am taken in turn.
Hunted and hunter,
Prey and predator,
Blood to blood,
Bone to bone,
Hide to skin,
And skin to hide,
Protector and protected,
We stand together and apart:
Pack-mate* to pack-mate*,
I call you companion;
Pack-mate* to pack-mate*,
I stand behind you;
Pack-mate* to pack-mate*,
I stand in front;
I stand beside.
Hunter and hunted,
Predator and prey.

*Flock-fellow, Litter-mate (in the case of
animals such as cats, beaver, etc.) or Herd-kin
may be substituted where more applicable.*

DECEMBER 6

Here I lay this honey sweet,
For those of Mound, Sky, and Wild;
With the Huntsmen, sword and bond to ride:
For my heart is of my Ancestors
Who with you now reside.
Huntsmen, hear my call!
I sound the horn of my heart,
For it beats pure:
Be near me now;
Surround me now!
Huntsmen, hear my call!
Among you, let me stand:
Horn to dagger, hand-in-hand.
For my heart is of my Ancestors,
And I heed their call to ride!

December 7

Spirit of the Vardhmadhr,
Who has been set to guard
My space,
My home,
My person,
And those whom I hold dear:
From *fjandar*,
From ill-meaning wights,
From those who mean to do us harm:
For your guardianship,
I blot you:
You, who actively defend me.
For your sacrifice for my protection,
I lay this offering,
And I toast you:
To your health,
To your welfare,
To your strength!
May you be hail and welcome
In my home and at my hearth!
Skal!

DECEMBER 8

I place the goat
Upon my altar;
Hammer-sign,
To honor Thor.
Julbocken
Made of straw,
Bedecked with red.
I place the goat
Upon my altar;
Kiss its horns,
To honor Jord.
Julbocken
Made of straw,
Bedecked with red.
I place the goat
Upon my altar;
Kick its heels,
To remember what's restored.
Julbocken
Made of straw,
Bedecked with red.
I place the goat
Upon my altar;
Three taps upon its little head:
Bless the year past;
Bless this moment;
Bless the year ahead.

DECEMBER 9

Cattle die, friends die,
One dies oneself the same,
But fame never dies,
For him who gains righteousness for himself.

Cattle die, friends die,
One dies oneself the same,
I know one that never dies:
Renown of the dead.

I pour this glass
For the Righteous;
I raise this glass
For the Renowned Dead.
I drink this glass
For my Ancestors;
I leave this glass:
Through my honor,
May they never die.

--Portions from *Havamal* 76-77, translation mine.

DECEMBER 10

I light this candle
Upon my stalli-shelf;
May it glow brightly
To light the way
Of Ancestor and Alf.
All those Good Ones
Gone before,
I honor you this night,
And in the Season
Soon to come:
Yule, Blessed and Bright.
Let there ever be
Peace between
Thee and me.
Peace and good seasons to you,
And to those who have come before,
And to those who will come after.
Blessed be.

DECEMBER 11

I light this candle
Upon my stalli-shelf;
May it glow brightly
To light the way
Of Nisse and Tomte.
All those Husvaettir
In nook and doorway,
I honor you this night,
And in the Season
Soon to come:
Yule, Blessed and Bright.
Let there ever be
Peace between
Thee and me.
Peace and good seasons to you,
And to those who have come before,
And to those who will come after.
Blessed be.

DECEMBER 12

I light this candle
Upon my stalli-shelf;
May it glow brightly
To light the way
Of Huldrafolk
And Landvaettir.
All you spirits of the Land,
I honor you this night,
And in the Season
Soon to come:
Yule, Blessed and Bright.
Let there ever be
Peace between
Thee and me.
Peace and good seasons to you,
And to those who have come before,
And to those who will come after.
Blessed be.

DECEMBER 13

I light this candle
Upon my stalli-shelf;
May it glow brightly
To light the way
Of Aesir and Vanir.
All You Shining Gods
Of Yore,
I honor You this night,
And in the Season
Soon to come:
Yule, Blessed and Bright.
Let there ever be
Peace between
Thee and me.
Peace and good seasons to you,
And to those who have come before,
And to those who will come after.
Blessed be.

DECEMBER 14

I light this candle
Upon my stalli-shelf;
May it glow brightly
To light the way
Of the Proud Rokkr.
All You Gods of Twilight,
Of Time, and of Comfort,
I honor You this night,
And in the Season
Soon to come:
Yule, Blessed and Bright.
Let there ever be
Peace between
Thee and me.
Peace and good seasons to you,
And to those who have come before,
And to those who will come after.
Blessed be.

DECEMBER 15

I light this candle
Upon my stalli-shelf;
May it glow brightly
To light the way
Of the Sun's return.
Hail, Bright Sunna;
Come anew!
I honor You this night,
And in the Season
Soon to come:
Yule, Blessed and Bright.
Let there ever be
Peace between
Thee and me.
Peace and good seasons to you,
And to those who have come before,
And to those who will come after.
Blessed be.

DECEMBER 16

Well is to cauldron
As cauldron to cup:
Stir the cauldron thrice.
Urdh is to Midgard
As Midgard to Urdh:
Stir the cauldron thrice.
Once for Urdr:
That which became;
Was-and-is-and-was.
Once for Verdhandi:
That which becomes;
Will be-and-is-and-will be.
Once for Skuld:
That which shall be;
The Wyrd of yet-to-come.
Well is to cauldron
As cauldron to cup:
Stir the cauldron thrice.
To the Norns
This blot I give.
Stir the cauldron thrice.
Cup run over;
Pour again!
Stir the cauldron thrice.
Weave a Wyrd
That's fair to live.
Stir the cauldron thrice.
Cup run over;
Pour again!
Stir the cauldron thrice.

YULE

DECEMBER 17

Here stands Baldur for whom mead is brewed,
Bright-clear powerful, a shield laid over,
But the power of the Gods is a prideful spirit.
Hodhr bears the tall fateful-branch thither,
He shall be the death of Your Baldur
And Odin's son deprive of life.

Baldur's dreams were baleful.
Long His nights, and weary.
Lo, the ache of doom,
When knowing is worse than not.
Thus All-Father rode to Helheim,
And Frigga took the oaths
Of every leaf and tree and twig;
Droplet, shrub, and stone.
Fire would spare, and water;
Metal would spare, and rock.
Sickness would spare, and weapon;
Wild beasts and birds and poison asp:
All would spare Her Son.
Except the mistletoe was young:
She thought it too innocent to swear.

--Portions from *Baldurs Draumar*, my translation

YULE

DECEMBER 18

White berries on the altar:
Let me not give in to pride.
White berries on the altar:
Help me heal my Shadow side.
White berries on the altar:
Words and insults will not wound.
White berries on the altar:
My self-esteem will not be bruised.
White berries on the altar:
Oath of Frigga, I invoke.
Let me harm not others,
Lest I myself be harmed.
Instead,
Let me seek Justice
For both the weak
And the strong.
And should I do harm unknowingly,
Let it be put to Right
By the Gods' own Power,
And by the Gods' own Might.
Enda er, ok enda skal vera.

(I *do not recommend* the use of *real* mistletoe for
this blessing! I am well aware that there are many
readers out there—perhaps even yourself—who will
make an ugly face at the very thought of *plastic*
berries, but the fact remains: they're ultimately
safer than their natural alternative. If you have
small children or pets with access to your stalli,
even *plastic* berries should be disposed of/put away
immediately afterwards.)

YULE

DECEMBER 19

Loki,
Teach me laughter
At my own mistakes.
Sigyn,
Provide shelter
From all of life's heartaches.
Hela,
Hold the door
For my Ancestors
As they walk this night,
That they may
Come to call and visit me
On the cusp
Of bright Yuletide.
I raise a cup
To the Rokkr:
The Gods of the Twilight.
May frith be kept
Between us,
As we work side by side.
Peace and good seasons to You and Yours;
Peace and good seasons to me.
In return for blessings given,
A gift for a gift
These blessings be.

YULE

DECEMBER 20

Mothers,
May I dance!
Mothers,
May I sing!
Mothers,
May I thank the Gods
For each new day
Dawn brings!
I raise my voice
On Mother's Night:
Hail, Modra!
Hail to the Disir,
Dark and Bright;
Mothers
Who Have Come Before;
Mothers
Who Are Sister-Wights!
Hail, Modra!
Hail also to the Asynjur:
Aesir, Vanir, and Rokkr!
Mother, Sister, Daughter, Wife:
Godly Women,
Bless my life!
Hail, Modra!
Mothers,
May I dance!
Mothers,
May I sing!
Mothers,
May I thank the Gods
For every goodly thing!

YULE

DECEMBER 21

Radiant Baldur,
I give you my tears
That they may shine
Instead of drown my feeble heart.
Teach me to be impenetrable;
Skin-hardened,
Yet heart-bright.
Make of me a beacon
To shine in the darkness
Of this world,
And all others.
Radiant Baldur,
Shining One:
Remind me on this
Longest night
Of the promise of
Returning day;
That every end
Is but a new beginning.
Radiant Baldur,
God of the Shining Day:
Show me Your face
That I may know hope;
That hope may know me.

YULE

DECEMBER 22

By your Hallowed Names,
I charge this rune:
Ansuz.
Odin's Rune;
God-Rune;
Rune of blessings spoken.
Sign of communication and inspiration;
Of Wisdom and Truth.
I carve you thus;
With your help, I advise against vanity,
    manipulation, and misunderstanding.
I paint you the purple of the royal Aesir;
I prove you through wise words, clear
    communication, inspired speech, and blessings
    bestowed.
I pray you: *Bless*.
I blot you with poetry and the blessing of others.
I send you forth as inspiration, wisdom, and
    blessings for myself;
Inspiration, wisdom, and blessings for those I hold
    dear.

YULE

DECEMBER 23

Hallowed by thy shape
I stand:
Feet planted firm,
With outstretched hands.
Mjollnir,
Hammer of the Gods,
By thy sign
I am made *hlaut*.
Set apart
To do Gods' work;
Spirit-touched,
Though bound to Earth.
Hammer-kiss
Upon my brow
That wisdom
Shape both oath and vow.
Hammer-kiss
Upon my heart
That I be loyal,
Brave, and true
To those I love and to the Tru.
Hammer-kiss
Upon my lips
To keep me honest:
Tame my tongue.
Hallowed by thy shape
I stand:
Feet planted firm,
With outstretched hands.

YULE

DECEMBER 24

All-Father:
Hanging on the windy Tree,
Gungnir buried deep,
You bled for wisdom.
Standing by the Well of Urdh,
You sealed the deal
And said the words;
With outstretched hand
You gave the gift
Of your own eye
For wisdom.
Lord,
Let me not share your thirst;
Let me know when well
Is well enough.
Give me just enough
To do Your work,
And I promise
To be grateful.

YULE

DECEMBER 25

I know You hung on the windy tree,
Nights all nine,
Wounded by the point of Your own spear;
Self sacrificed to Self.
None made You happy then,
With loaf or with horn:
I offer bread and mead to You;
Look down upon me;
Gift me the runes.
Let me howl for You and to You;
I fall to my knees in respect.
Teach me the mighty songs
Of Your Grandfather
As You drink this mundane mead;
Replace it, I pray, with the Mead of Poetry.
Let me be awash in wisdom;
May I grow well and begin to thrive.
Word by word, may I seek words;
Deed by deed, may I seek righteous deeds.
Runes may I find, and advising symbols:
Teach me how to carve them;
Teach me how to use them to advise.
Teach me how to paint them;
Teach me how to prove them in my life.
Teach me how to pray them;
Teach me how to blot.
Teach me how to send them,
And how to draw them back.
A gift looks for a gift:
Yet let me not over-sacrifice;
Let me not ask too much.

--Inspired by *Havamal* 138-144, translation mine

YULE

DECEMBER 26

Hail Heimdall!
Friend of Humanity,
White Watchman of All:*
Guard and guide us,
To set a Watch over our own lives,
That we may be fair and inclusive,
Recognizing differences as the core
Of what creates a society.
Keep us focused on our goals,
Even in times of great turmoil;
Even as Gjallahorn echoes
Across the ages of Time.
Help us to stand in defense
Of what You have made
True and Right:
Though this person be different from that one,
All begin as worthy in the sight of the Gods.
Help us help them remain so.
Make of us builders of bridges;
Breathers of rainbows.
Son of Nine Mothers,
Remind us:
Every person is some Mother's
Daughter or Son.
With your able help,
I set my Watch,
And let it not be ended
'Til right be done.

*White Watchman is a traditional by-name of Heimdall,
wherein White implies "Bright and Good, not "caucasian"!

YULE

DECEMBER 27

Golden tables in the grass:
Those ones which in days of yore belonged to the
  Aesir.
Set a place for me!
There will be many well-sown fields to grow,
Disasters shall all get better, Baldur will come.
Let me plow those fields!
Come, Baldur, come!
Hoenir shall choose the sacred twig,
And the Sons of Odin shall dwell in Vanaheim.
Help me, Hoenir:
To make a wand for this year and years after.
Let me likewise look to the West.
There comes in the kingdom such mighty spells,
Powerful from above, from He who counsels
  everyone.
Hail to Baldur's mighty spells!
Counsel me, God of the Shining Day:
Teach me magick that restores and heals;
Magick that blesses homes and fields;
Magick that makes Justice grow,
As sprouts fighting upwards 'gainst earth and snow.
Come, Baldur, come!
I greet You gift for gift:
Mead and honey,
Bread and milk.
Come, Baldur, come!

--Portions from *Voluspa* 61-66, translation mine

YULE

DECEMBER 28

At Season's close,
I raise my wand:
Hail to what has been before,
And to what is,
And to what comes after.
Bless the seasons yet-to-come
With Yule's companionship and laughter:
With family gathered round me,
And friends at my door;
Let me work throughout the year
Upon the lessons I have learned at Yule.
Hail to Baldur and to Odin;
Hail to Heimdall and to Hoenir!
I raise a glass and pour this blot
To all of You and Thor:
Draw the Hammer,
Hallow; Bless.
Let my life be Mjollnir-kissed!
Let my work be likewise blessed,
As I go forward from this Yule.

DECEMBER 29

By your Hallowed Names,
I charge this rune:
Mannaz.
Mani's Rune;
Mankind's Rune;
Rune of The Self and the individual.
Sign of friends and enemies; of social order;
Of strong opinions, intelligence, Divinity, and
    trusted assistance.
I carve you thus;
With your help, I advise against depression,
    delusion, cunning, and manipulation.
I paint you the blue and purple of the phases of the
    moon;
I prove you each time I act on my own behalf, voice
    my own opinion, or otherwise celebrate my own
    individuality.
I pray you: *I* .
I blot you by honoring the phases of the moon, my
    Ancestors, and the Alfar.
I send you forth as individuality and self-esteem for
    myself;
Individuality and self-esteem for those I hold dear.

DECEMBER 30

Hail Rig!
You who strides the middle-road,
To walk amongst Mankind;
Heimdall in a different guise
Who Purpose and Magick bestows.
Help me choose my Path:
The Path which is my Purpose;
That One which I was born to walk,
And born to do.
Make my back strong,
If I am to be a hard-worker;
If I am to plow the fields,
Let them not be strewn with rocks.
Make my mind keen,
If I am to be a yeoman:
If I am to take a job as merchant,
Or headhunter, or in a professional skill.
Make my heart wise,
If I am to be a leader or magickian;
If others are to follow me,
Or look to me for counsel,
Keep me kind.
Help me choose my Path:
The Path which is my Purpose;
That One which I was born to walk,
And born to do.

December 31

O! My Gods and Good Wights!
Gift me with a Purpose-Driven Life:
Let me be a person who makes a difference.
Show me that even the smallest of us
Can change worlds;
That nothing is trivial.
Help me to know my Self,
That I may better undertand others.
For:
Even the lame ride horses,
Herds are driven by the handless,
The deaf earn glory and show prowess,
To be blind is better than to be burned,
A corpse is good for nothing.
Set me to reach further;
To reach higher;
To always seek the common ground--
The middle-way--
Where Justice is done,
And wrongs are righted.
Even in the smallest ways,
Make of me a force for change.
For even You Gods know:
Change is necessary.

--Portions from *Havamal* 71, translation mine.

JANUARY 1

Fehu Uruz Thurisaz
Ansuz Raidho
Kenaz Gebo Wunjo.
Hail Freyja, Vanadis!
Valfreyja,
Gefn,
She who is Odin's Third Teacher,
Mother-of-Seidhr!
Skal!
Reveal for me
The Farmer-Healer's Aett:
Cattle low gently
The promise of wealth;
Let it pass to and through and to.
Horns lowered,
The ox bears
The strength of mountains.
Thunder roll above the thorns
Bringing change and
Regeneration.
Bless the Gods bless me!
The road yet is long,
But I see the promise of new horizons.
Fire manifests fire.
Gift for gift
I shall repay
And be repaid.
Thus: Bliss.
Fehu Uruz Thurisaz
Ansuz Raidho
Kenaz Gebo Wunjo.

JANUARY 2

Hagalaz
Nauthiz Isa
Jera
Eihwaz Perdhro
Algiz
Sowilo.
Hail Heimdall! White-God;
Bridge-Guardian;
Horn-Blower who warns against destruction;
Leader of Odin's bright retinue;
Son of the Nine Mothers!
Skal!
Reveal for me
The Yeoman-Warrior's Aett:
Hail warns of destruction and loss
In harmony.
I find myself in need;
Resistance leads to strength.
Ice reminds me to be still.
Cycles bring change bring harvest and reward.
I am strong as the Yew is strong;
Trustworthy, dependable, and ready to defend.
I unravel mysteries.
Shield-sign shelters and protects.
Sunna rises even in the midst of great change.
Hagalaz
Nauthiz Isa
Jera
Eihwaz Perdhro
Algiz
Sowilo.

JANUARY 3

Tiwaz
Berkano Ehwaz Mannaz
Laguz
Inguz
Dagaz
Othala.
Hail Tyr! Oath-Keeper;
You who are called "Leavings of the Wolf";
Justice-Bringer;
Law-Giver;
Thing-Ruler!
Skal!
Reveal for me
The Priest-King's Aett:
Honorable self-sacrifice
Often leads to Justice.
The birch boasts of rebirth.
It is always worse for the horse,
Than for the rider.
Mani looks over the whole of Mankind.
Water flows, heals, and grows:
Be water, my friend.
Freyr blesses those with common sense.
Each day burns bright with opportunity.
Such is our heritage.
Tiwaz
Berkano Ehwaz Mannaz
Laguz
Inguz
Dagaz
Othala.

JANUARY 4

Underground
I go
Within.
I am
Seed
Planted.
Inside
I am the
Dead
Yet
Living:
The long thread
Left by my
Ancestors.
And I
Pull
That thread:
Guide me
Through the
Labyrinth.
Volundarhus:
I circle
Seven times.
I lay a blot of
Seven rings for
Volundr and
Freyja:
Lead me on this path
Underground.

JANUARY 5

Hail Volundr!
Hail to the Dis-Wed
Smith of Vegeance and Peace!
Hail to the Winged Man,
King of the Alfar,
Alongside Freyr!
I pass in a circle
Seven times:
One for each year
Shared with your Beloved,
Wise Hervor Alvitr.
I lay rings
In blot to you;
Pour red wine
To remember
Blood-spilled reckoning.
Feathers upon my stalli:
May you ever
Keep your wings.
Teach me to soar;
To laugh as I fly,
Rising above
Those who would
Deign to bind me
To my Shadow.

January 6

Hail Vanadis!
Lady of the Labyrinth,
Keep my steps sure.
Wise Freyja,
I bring gifts
For Gefn:
Amber,
To catch my tears;
Rose quartz,
For the mystery
Of Lover and Beloved:
What lies between.
Guide me to the center
Of my Self.
Teach me not to fear
The Shadow,
But yet learn its lessons.
Seven times,
I circle:
What do these pieces of me mean?
Seeker
Maker
Believer
Dreamer
Peacemaker
Lover
Mystic:
I lie somewhere between.
Find me.

JANUARY 7

Seeker:
Ask the Question;
Find the Answer.
Outside
Looking in:
Follow the thread.
Vanadis,
Am I this?
Guide me to the
Center of My Truth:
(Here, pull a rune)
(Interpret the rune)
(Apply it to yourself as Seeker,
Or not.)
Forth from the Labyrinth
I shall go;
Thread unravel;
Knowledge grow.
A gift for a gift:
Blot I pour
For Vanadis:
Hail Holy Hörn!

JANUARY 8

Maker:
To be both Artist
And the Art.
Outside
Looking in:
Follow the thread.
Vanadis,
Am I this?
Guide me to the
Center of My Truth:
(Here, pull a rune)
(Interpret the rune)
(Apply it to yourself as Maker,
Or not.)
Forth from the Labyrinth
I shall go;
Thread unravel;
Knowledge grow.
A gift for a gift:
Blot I pour
For Vanadis:
Hail Holy Hörn!

JANUARY 9

Believer:
All is All;
Belief, Hope, and Charity.
Outside
Looking in:
Follow the thread.
Vanadis,
Am I this?
Guide me to the
Center of My Truth:
(Here, pull a rune)
(Interpret the rune)
(Apply it to yourself as Believer,
Or not.)
Forth from the Labyrinth
I shall go;
Thread unravel;
Knowledge grow.
A gift for a gift:
Blot I pour
For Vanadis:
Hail Holy Hörn!

JANUARY 10

Dreamer:
Dare to Dream;
Dream to Dare.
Outside
Looking in:
Follow the thread.
Vanadis,
Am I this?
Guide me to the
Center of My Truth:
(Here, pull a rune)
(Interpret the rune)
(Apply it to yourself as Dreamer,
Or not.)
Forth from the Labyrinth
I shall go;
Thread unravel;
Knowledge grow.
A gift for a gift:
Blot I pour
For Vanadis:
Hail Holy Hörn!

JANUARY 11

Peacemaker:
Problems are Opportunities
For Compassionate Response.
Outside
Looking in:
Follow the thread.
Vanadis,
Am I this?
Guide me to the
Center of My Truth:
(Here, pull a rune)
(Interpret the rune)
(Apply it to yourself as Peacemaker,
Or not.)
Forth from the Labyrinth
I shall go;
Thread unravel;
Knowledge grow.
A gift for a gift:
Blot I pour
For Vanadis:
Hail Holy Hörn!

JANUARY 12

Lover:
Lover and Beloved
And what lies between.
Outside
Looking in:
Follow the thread.
Vanadis,
Am I this?
Guide me to the
Center of My Truth:
(Here, pull a rune)
(Interpret the rune)
(Apply it to yourself as Lover,
Or not.)
Forth from the Labyrinth
I shall go;
Thread unravel;
Knowledge grow.
A gift for a gift:
Blot I pour
For Vanadis:
Hail Holy Hörn!

JANUARY 13

Mystic:
Self is not sole,
But Soul.
Outside
Looking in:
Follow the thread.
Vanadis,
Am I this?
Guide me to the
Center of My Truth:
(Here, pull a rune)
(Interpret the rune)
(Apply it to yourself as Mystic,
Or not.)
Forth from the Labyrinth
I shall go;
Thread unravel;
Knowledge grow.
A gift for a gift:
Blot I pour
For Vanadis:
Hail Holy Hörn!

January 14

(Insert THREE of the archetypes from the past
seven days; Example:
Seeker, Maker, Believer)
My feet are on the ground;
I stand firm.
I am of the earth and the earth is of me;
I stand firm.
I center myself, and I hold.
Enda er, ok enda skal vera.
Enda er, ok enda skal vera.
Enda er, ok enda skal vera.
I come up from the Deep;
I crawl out from the Labyrinth.
See my face
Sun
See Your own;
See them both as one:
Shining,
Like Heidhr.
Standing firm,
Bright Witch I be:
I know myself to know Thee.
Enda er, ok enda skal vera.
Enda er, ok enda skal vera.
Enda er, ok enda skal vera.

JANUARY 15

I celebrate myself,
And all that is me.
Bright thoughts;
Quick-minded
Hugr.
Memory and Legacy
Intertwine:
Hamingja.
My shape may not be
Your ideal of me,
But it is mine:
Hamr
Strong and lithe
To fare-forth.
Wyrd shapes me,
As I shape my Wyrd:
Fylgja,
Follow close.
I celebrate myself,
And all that is me.

January 16

I pour this blot
For Loki:
Hail Silver-Tongue!
Teach me to accept
Those things
Which are beyond
My control.
Help me learn
To laugh
At myself,
Yet also to
Take responsibility
For my mistakes.
Let there be peace
Between me and Thee;
Ever uphold frith.
Let not disaster or catastrophe
Pin my wings
Nor paint my life
With Shadow.
Hail Loki!

JANUARY 17

Adaptable:
Let me be water.
You put water in a cup;
It becomes the cup.
Let me be soft;
Changing my shape
When necessary.
Yet hard,
As water as it
Aches against rock.
Njordr,
Teach me the lessons
Of peace-keeping:
To find the middle ground,
No matter the horizon.
Let me pour out
Rum for you,
And seawater.
Teach me to reach
As waves reach
Ever toward
Further shores.

JANUARY 18

I am the lineage
Of my Ancestors:
Blood and bone
Woven into me.
I honor you.
I am the love
Of my Ancestors:
Nurturing kin,
Adopted and born-to,
Burning within.
I honor you.
I am the spirit
Of my Ancestors:
All those who birthed
The Path
Manifest through me.
I honor you.
I am the story
Of my Ancestors:
Inspirations and dreams
Enacted by me.
I honor you.
I am the home
Of my Ancestors:
In this place
They once called home.
I honor you.
Peace and good seasons to you,
And to all those who came before,
And to all those who will come after.
Blessed be.

JANUARY 19

I was
Weak
But learned
To be strong;
Lost,
But my Gods
Found me.
I was
Hopeless
But learned
To depend;
Defenseless,
But learned
To fight.
I was
Confused,
But I found
Reason;
Tired,
But I endured.
I was
Shiftless,
But I found
Drive;
Questioning
Til I found
Truth.

JANUARY 20

Raudh-Gull,
Freyja;
Red-Gold:
Help me
Understand
My own power.
Remind me
That I create
My own reality.
Let me make it
Passionate!
May my world
Burn
With the fires
Of inspiration--
Always.
Light a fire
Within
To manifest
Make manifest
Be manifested.
Hail Holy Hörn!
Fire-Woman;
Bright Heidhr,
Hail!

JANUARY 21

Ingvi-Freyr:
Light-Bringer!
In the heart of winter,
Hear my call!
Accept these gifts,
And know my love
For You
And all that You bring:
Self-knowledge
Of a kind
That teaches
Common sense;
That breathes
Warmth
Into relationships:
Familial and romantic.
Help me to
Love
My work,
And also to
Understand:
Love is
Work.

JANUARY 22

Like the oak
I reach out
My arms to
Freedom.
Rooted
In
Faith;
Planted
On
Earth.
Strong
I am;
Sure and
True.
Like the oak
I reach up
My arms to
Sky;
Touch
Gods.

JANUARY 23

Back bent
Under the strain
Of worries and woes
I groan forward,
Knowing You are with me.
Thrudh Thorsdottir:
Hail and well met,
And blessings to You.
Teach me
The strength of mountains;
Power,
As rock as it aches against water.
Make me;
Make me over:
Into proud aurochs;
Strong ox,
Yet not
Over-stubborn.
A bit of backbone
Heals
When
Back bends
Under strain.

JANUARY 24

Hail Tyr!
Thing-Ruler,
Law-Giver;
You,
Who are called
"Leavings of the Wolf":
Here,
Blot
I pour out
For all You have
Given me, and
Yet will give.
Integrity
You have taught me;
Honor;
To be Just and Right.
When lost
Inside
My own pain,
You have
Understood, and
Understand.
Hail Tyr!
Thing-Ruler,
Law-Giver:
You of Outstretched-Hand.
Skal!

JANUARY 25

Gifts have I been
Given;
The best of these:
Myself.
A gift for a gift
I give
Myself
Back again to
Gods and
Humankind.
Let me
Live this life
To its
Fullest;
Eke out
Every ounce of
Living;
Each breath:
A gift.
I return my
Breath
To the trees;
My heart
To those in
Need of it.

JANUARY 26

At the foot of Yggdrasil,
My heart set forth to walk:
To worlds and between,
It set forth to go,
Knowledge to gain,
And friends to know.
Midgard-Realm to Vanaheim,
Golden-fielded Folkvangr;
Seabirds called along the coasts of Helheim's shore.
I left my offerings at Gastropnir;
Poured blot to Menglodh Fair,
And at day's end I found myself
At the foot of the Spiral Stair.
From Svartalfheim-deep
To Asgard-high,
My hamr travelled there,
And when I woke
From sleep-not-sleep,
I found myself not wearied.
For though I travelled far and deep,
In wonders had I gloried.

JANUARY 27

My shape
Is more
Than the bend
Of my back;
The crook
Of my knees.
More than
The lines of
My face;
The whorls
Of fingerprints.
Hamr-strong:
My shape
Is soul-and-more:
Thoughts
Hands
Legacy
Heart.
I cannot change
The way
That you may
See me;
Only the way
In which
I know
Myself.

JANUARY 28

A season
Is drawing
To a close,
And I look
Westward
Once again,
Toward
Vanaheim.
Hear the heartbeat
Of pounding hooves;
Waving fields
Of wheat
And promises.
The Lady
Bends Her
Hand
To touch this
Wintered heart.
Hail Vanadis,
Upon Your seat
In Sessrumnir.
Save a seat for me.

JANUARY 29

By your Hallowed Names,
I charge this rune:
Ehwaz.
Sleipnir's Rune;
Horse-Rune;
Rune of transportation and travel.
Sign of movement and change;
Of teamwork and partnerships.
I carve you thus;
With your help, I advise against reckless haste,
    betrayal, and confinement.
I paint you the red and white of chestnuts and
    greys;
I prove you each time I work well in a team with
    others; each time I make a change for the better,
    no matter how gradual my progress.
I pray you: *Together*.
I blot you with images of horses and with
    sweetgrass and oats.
I send you forth as loyalty, trust, and fair travels for
    myself;
Loyalty, trust, and fair travels for those I hold dear.

JANUARY 30

Grey-maned
Sleipnir
I blot
With clear water,
Oats, and grain:
Carry me,
Carry me,
Carry me
Away:
Down,
Down:
Into the Grey;
To Helheim shore
With roaring waves;
Crying gulls
Cry
Ancestral names
Of that long and storied
Maternal line
That's gone before:
Mothers,
Daughters,
Sisters,
Friends.
Bring me to ride,
Among these
Brave women,
Who shaped me
In wombs of
Hearts and thoughts.

JANUARY 31

Together
Never
Torn apart:
Dawn of Disablot
Reminds us
Of memories
Precious
And lessons
Learned.
Mother's touch;
Sister's laugh:
Regained;
Remembered.
I am
All those
Women
Who made me who
I am,
Whether
I am
Woman or
I am
Not.

Disablot

February 1

Hail Disir!
Blessings and Honor
To You and Your kin,
And to any of my own kin
Who have come to serve You.
Blessings and Honor
To the Disir:
To those who once walked beside us,
As our Ancestors and kin,
And to those who never did,
But are among us, just the same.
Peace and good seasons to you,
And may there ever be frith between us,
And between me and mine,
And those who have come before and who will
    come after.
For all that you have done for us,
And for all that you will do;
For all that you have meant to us,
And for all that you will mean:
Peace and good seasons;
Love, gratitude, and honor.
Blessed be!

DISABLOT

FEBRUARY 2

Hail Modra!
Hail to the Mothers;
Called by others
Matronae,
Matres.
Hail!
Handmaidens of Frigga,
Bright Asynjur;
Queens in Asgard,
Vanaheim,
Helheim;
Even Jotunheim.
Hail!
Hail Valkyrjur!
Handmaidens of Odin,
Swan-maids;
Members of Freyja's
Bright retinue!
Hail!
Hail Disir!
Ancestors and Fylgjur;
Bright Maids and Dark.
Hail!
Blot for you:
Gift for gift,
For all that
Has been given,
And all still
Yet to give!

DISABLOT

FEBRUARY 3

A season closes
In the dark of
Winter's night:
One last pouring
Of wine and salt;
One last offering
Of bread and sweets.
What was begun
At Winternights
We now seal;
Another turning
Of the Wheel.
Hail and Farewell,
Bright Disir,
Yet do not
Wander far;
Rather, remain
Ever-close,
Reminding us
Who we are,
Who we have been, and
Who we yet will be.
A season closes
In the dark of
Winter's night:
One last pouring
Of wine and salt;
One last offering
Of bread and sweets.
Hail Disir!

FEBRUARY 4

By your Hallowed Names,
I charge this rune:
Isa.
Skadi's Rune;
Ice-Rune;
Rune of challenges and frustrations.
Sign of standstills and times to turn inward;
Of introspection and holding fast.
I carve you thus;
With your help, I advise against treachery, illusion,
    deceit, and betrayal.
I paint you ice-white and shimmering;
I prove you by standing still and seeking clarity.
I pray you: *Be Still.*
I blot you with ice and snow-water.
I send you forth as stillness and the ability to hold
    fast for myself;
Stillness and the ability to hold fast for those I hold
    dear.

FEBRUARY 5

Introspection
Breeds
Inspiration:
Fire burns in the head.
Drink me deep
Of the Mead of Poetry:
Blood of Kvasir.
Raise the glass
For Odin;
Raise the glass
Again!
Raise the glass
For Bragi,
And give Him
His Full!*
Open the way;
Stoke the flame!
Drink me deep
Of the Mead of Poetry:
Blood of Kvasir.

Full: a toast; as in respect.

FEBRUARY 6

Words can heal;
Words can harm:
The tongue is the killer housed in the head.
May my words
Build and bless;
Bring illumination
To the distressed.
May they be laced
With Justice;
Work towards
Righteousness.
May they bind me
To my oaths;
Keep me loyal
Among the host.
May they not blight
My Hamingja,
But build a Legacy
That prides even
The Gods.
Words can heal;
Words can harm:
The tongue is the killer housed in the head.
Give me the power
The tongue to tame,
For that is the best
Sort of wisdom I could claim.

--Portions from *Havamal* 73, translation mine.

FEBRUARY 7

Speak plainly,
Write slowly;
Teach clearly,
Advise gently.
Words flower;
Flow-not-crash.
Dream-speaker:
My language
Bounds Otherworlds
In thoughts and rhymes.
Spirit-speaker:
My language
Keeps Ancestors alive.
Priest-speaker:
My language
Gifts the Gods.
Plain-speaker:
I am as good as my word.

FEBRUARY 8

Hail Thor!
Plain-Speaker,
Mjollnir-Wielder,
Protect us in the storms of life;
Help us to speak plainly
And with Honesty,
Even to ourselves.
Let word be bond,
And oath be hallowed:
Mjollnir-kissed.
Teach me to treasure
Simplicity.
Let thunder roar
And wave crash,
Yet not the words
Falling from my tongue.
If I cannot say something nice,
Put Your great arm
Around my shoulders,
And Your hammer-holding hand
Over my mouth.

FEBRUARY 9

By your Hallowed Names,
I charge this rune:
Thurisaz.
Thor's Rune;
Thorn-Rune;
Jotun-Rune;
Rune of reactive force and will.
Sign of change and regeneration;
Of cleansing fire, destruction, and defense.
I carve you thus;
With your help, I advise against danger, betrayal,
    malice, and lies.
I paint you the red of burning flames;
I prove you through directed force of will; through
    sexual energy and acceptance of change.
I pray you: *Protect*.
I blot you with fire and incense.
I send you forth as protection and regeneration for
    myself;
Protection and regeneration for those I hold dear.

FEBRUARY 10

Fire
Cleanse
This space;
Fire
Hold
This space;
Fire
Heal
This space.
Fire
Make
This space
Hlaut:
Set apart;
Sacred.
Fire
Defend
This space;
Fire
Protect
This space;
Fire
Make
This space
Hlaut:
Set apart;
Sacred.
Enda er, ok enda skal vera.
Enda er, ok enda skal vera.
Enda er, ok enda skal vera.

FEBRUARY 11

Blackbird, blackbird,
Camouflage;
Change--
Take a message
To your Master:
The harsh wind
Does not break
The strong tree;
It can only be swayed.
Hail Loki,
Master of Change!
Fall black feathers
Round about.
Red-winged blackbird,
Sit and sing;
To your Master,
Galdr bring.
Birdish magicks
Of flight and flyt,
Sweep me up
This blessed night.
Loki teach me:
Camouflage;
Change:
The harsh wind
Does not break
The strong tree;
It can only be swayed.

FEBRUARY 12

Audhumbla lows.
Ice,
Fire,
Salt,
Blood:
Primal mist of Ginnungagap;
Audhumbla lows
And feeds the Giant.
Ice,
Fire,
Salt,
Blood:
Ymir's primal scream
As the world is born
From torn flesh
And hewn bone.
Ice,
Fire,
Salt,
Blood:
Audhumbla lows.

FEBRUARY 13

Wind sweeps
A darkening sky;
One sweet star.
Black fingered trees
Echo my skeleton
To the sky.
I am made real
In this:
One fractured moment
Of falling night.
Past,
Near forgot;
Present,
Escaping;
Future,
Not quite
Nor quiet.
Wyrd sweeps
A darkening sky;
One sweet star.
I am made real
In this:
One fractured moment
Of a falling night.

FEBRUARY 14

Vali:
Vengeance-Born
Justice-Bringer:
Teach me
To hold
Tightly
To those
And that
Which I
Love.
Gift for gift
Let me repay
What is
Gifted me:
Love for love;
Justice for injustice.
Remind me
You are
Not
A God of Death,
But of Life:
For Vengeance is
For the Living.
And then
Remind me
To live.

FEBRUARY 15

Ask and Embla
Ash and Vine:
Trees climb high
In one direction;
Every-which-way
Climbs
Vine.
Man and Woman
Woman to Man:
Both within,
Both without;
As above so below.
We are all
Twinned
Untwinned
Entwined:
Masculine and Feminine
Combined.
Embrace one half;
Embrace both.
Soul gives Odin;
Sense gives Hoenir,
And Lodhurr*, form.
Ask and Embla
Ash and Vine.

*Lodhurr: Many scholars, including John Lindow,
hold Lodhurr as another name for Loki.*

FEBRUARY 16

Move out
To move in;
Push
To pull.
We give
To take;
Take
To give.
Gift for gift:
Such is
Reciprocity.
To pray
For sun,
We must
Praise
The rain.
Nothing ventured;
Nothing gained.
To love
The warmth
We must
Brave
The cold.
Nothing ventured;
Nothing gained.
To give
The gift,
That gift must
First be
Poured out.

FEBRUARY 17

Aegishjalmur
Helm of Awe;
Helm of Aegir;
Helm of the Sea.
Algiz
Isa-Isa-Isa
Kenaz
Gebo
Protect and
Still;
Manifest
Gifts:
Of courage,
Strength,
Resolve.
Show me
The Warrior
Inside myself,
That I may
Stand proud
Against the
Backdrop of my
Ancestors.

FEBRUARY 18

My Truth
Is
Mine
And no one else's.
No one
Can
Take that
From me.
I step forward,
One hand open;
The other,
A fist:
One to console;
One to defend.
An offering:
Myself to myself;
Myself to the Gods.
Dead,
Yet I move.
I live
Between
To walk
Between.
Messenger, Lover;
Warrior, Sage.
I center myself,
And I hold.

FEBRUARY 19

I am mindful
Of my breath.
It flows through me,
And into the world.
I am mindful
Of my thoughts.
They flow through me,
And into the world.
I am mindful
Of my heart.
It flows through me,
And into the world.
I am mindful
Of my Gods.
They flow through me,
And into the world.
Let me be
As conscious
In community
As I am
Individually;
As aware of the
Needs
Of others,
As I am of my own
Breath.

FEBRUARY 20

Ours is the
Faith
Of the
Tribe:
Of a
People in
Community.
Let us
Never forget.
Skin
Doesn't matter:
We are
More
Than our
Skin.
Gender
Doesn't matter:
We are
All
Masculine;
Feminine;
Intertwined.
Creed
Only matters
When
It crushes
Others.
I will not be crushed;
I will not crush others.

FEBRUARY 21

Hail Njordr!
Peacemaking Navigator:
Help me
Navigate
Through life's
Stormy seas.
Show me
The bright horizons
Of shores
Covered in
Peace;
Covered in
Good and righteous deeds.
I paint Your rune:
Laguz.
I paint it a
Peaceful blue:
May there ever be
Peace
Between Thee and me;
May there ever be
Peace
Between me and mine;
May there ever be
Peace
Within as well as without;
May there ever be
Peace.

FEBRUARY 22

I am only
Human;
I make
Mistakes.
One thing
Mis-remembered
Does not
Make me
Less of
Who I am.
One stumble
Does not
Mean
I will always
Fall.
Gods
Likewise make
Mistakes;
They are not
Perfect:
Unexpected
Coffee-breaks
At the most
Inopportune of
Times.
Such is Wyrd;
Yet it keeps
Flowing,
As do I.

FEBRUARY 23

I reclaim
Viking:
Not for the
Sake of machismo
Or bravado;
Not as some
Masculine power trip,
But the
True meaning of
That word.
Let me be
One who dwells
By harbors
Of the mind
And of the heart,
Ready to launch
The ship of
Myself
Into the sea of
Possibility.
Let me be an
Explorer
Of long-forgotten
Worlds and
Opportunities.
Let me seek
New horizons,
Rather than
Dwelling in the
Past.

FEBRUARY 24

I am of the Land;
The Land is of me.
The wind upon my face
Is the breath of Gods;
Of Ancestors,
Breathed so long ago
Yet still alive;
Still blowing.
The earth is the ground
Of hallows cast
Ages past,
Yet still
Holy.
Birds speak,
And I hear Alfar.
Cattle low,
And Creation
Begins
Again and again.
Cycles and circles and me.
I am of the Land;
The Land is of me.

FEBRUARY 25

Awaken:
My heart yearns for
Coming Spring,
And I sing,
As birds call
Across snowy fields
And from leaf-bare trees.
Awaken:
Every sleeping bud
Beneath the earth
Beats the heart of
Landvaettir.
Awaken:
From hands not-mine
I reclaim that
Mis-begotten word:
Pagan.
Awaken:
I am of the Earth;
The Earth is of me,
For my Ancestors
Sleep within it;
I feed its thirst
With my blot.
Awaken:
I open my eyes
To see myself
In leaf and in tree;
In sky and in vine:
Limitless.

FEBRUARY 26

I cannot
Read
My life
In lines
On pages;
Cannot
Breathe
Against
Parchment
Locked between
Leather.
I am
Lurid-hued and
Living;
Color-swirled and
Faithbound;
Oathbound.
Locked between
Gods and Earth.
I cannot
Lead
My life
In lines
On pages;
Cannot
Breathe
Against
Parchment
Locked between
Leather.

FEBRUARY 27

Saga tells history,
Mystery;
Words of sages
And ages past.
Lore binds
And unbinds:
Words can imprison,
Or words can make us
Free.
I carve
Ansuz:
May I be
Blessed
With a story that is
Many-hued and
Painted bright.
I carve
Tiwaz:
May my tale be
True
And honorable,
Painted
In the broad strokes of
Justice-done.
I carve
Othala:
May my stories be a worthy
Inheritance, for:
Saga tells history.

FEBRUARY 28

Ice to Fire,
The Wheel
Turns,
And I am
Turning, too.
I have spent
Enough time
Within.
I raise my head;
Turn
To face the
Sun.
Ice to Fire,
The Wheel
Burns,
And I am
Burning, too.
I have spent
Enough time
Within.
I raise my heart;
Turn
To grow.

Ice to Fire,
The Wheel
Turns....

THE SEASON OF FIRE

SIGRBLOT, VANIRBLOT, MIDSUMMER, FREYRFAXI, WINTERNIGHTS

MARCH 1

I go walking
In the sunlight
Out under blue sky
The Landvaettir to know;
I go out walking
In the sunlight,
Searching for Truth.
I walk in circles
And in straight lines,
Finding gifts along the way;
A gift for a gift,
I go wight-walking.
Bless the walking and the finding;
The knowing and the minding
Of each Spirit that I find along my way.
Bless the walking and the finding;
The keeping and the binding
Of the sacred kinships that are formed
As I pass along the way.
I go walking
In the sunlight
Out under blue sky
The Landvaettir to know;
I go out walking
In the sunlight,
Searching for Truth.

MARCH 2

By your Hallowed Names,
I charge this rune:
Berkano.
Frigga's Rune;
Birch-Rune;
Rune of birth and liberation.
Sign of fertility and regeneration; Of renewal,
   prosperity, and love.
I carve you thus;
With your help, I advise against carelessness, loss
   of control, and stagnation.
I paint you the yellow and white of spring daisies;
I prove you each time I grow in new ways; each
   time I fall in love; each time I am renewed.
I pray you: *Renew.*
I blot you with fresh flowers, with birch bark, and
   with dew.
I send you forth as renewal, prosperity, and love for
   myself;
Renewal, prosperity, and love for those I hold dear.

MARCH 3

Help me fall in love
Again,
Or perhaps for the
First time,
With my Gods,
My Faith,
My Ancestors,
My Self;
This World
And The Nine.
Show me
Radiance,
Hope,
Happiness.
Teach me
Gratitude,
Hospitality,
Justice-in-community.
Let the love I learn
Pour out from me:
Paid forward
A thousand thousand times
In the name of Gods,
My Ancestors,
Humanity.

MARCH 4

The first blush of melting ice
Hail Skadi!
Shoots of grass peek up through snow
Hail Skadi!
Days grow warm at last
Hail Skadi!
And Farewell!
Melt the ice with blot poured
Sweet, upon the ground.
Cup raised in salutation;
Offering given with open heart,
Open hand,
Seeking mind.
As the Ancestors slip
Below
We remain grounded
On the surface,
As Skadi upon Her skis
Hurries Eastward,
Over ice to Gastropnir.

MARCH 5

I bend low
To tend the ve;
Hands cold,
From chill of fading winter.
I bend low
To tend the ve;
Clear the last ice
From newborn shoots,
Pushing themselves upward,
Toward the embrace of 'wakening
Sunna.
I bend low
To tend the ve;
Stones set for summer pouring:
I bless these stones,
Set them apart as sacred;
Make them *hlaut*.
I bend low
To tend the ve;
Listen, as I take a knee,
To birds and squirrels
Above me:
Singing; preparing; awake.
I bend low,
To tend the ve.

MARCH 6

Bless this good earth,
For it is already
Blessed:
Kissed by the feet
Of Landvaettir.
I walk sunwise
With smoke
To please the Gods:
Set this place as *hlaut*.
This place may be
Simple,
But I will heart-forge it
Into a palace
For the spirits of the land;
For the honoring of Ancestors;
For communing with Gods.
Hammer-hallowed,
Let it be ve to me and Thee;
Sacred space,
Full of offerings.
Enda er, ok enda skal vera.
Enda er, ok enda skal vera.
Enda er, ok enda skal vera.

MARCH 7

Dark-kissed eaves
Of budding trees
Ache against
Sun-dewed sky:
Raise the drum and dance!
Spring comes softly,
Seeping across the land;
Glacial.
Raise the drum and dance!
Sing runesong:
Fehu Kenaz Uruz Berkano
Uruz Berkano
Kenaz Berkano
Berkano!
Raise the drum and dance!
Breathe the rhythm
As the world gives birth
Again, again, again.
Raise the drum and dance!
Fehu Kenaz Uruz Berkano
Uruz Berkano
Kenaz Berkano
Berkano!

MARCH 8

Land, sea, and air,
I call upon the Landvaettir:
Stand with me;
Stand beside.
Soar above;
In peace reside.
'Tween Thee and me,
Let peace ever be;
Good seasons come
To me and those I love.
Rainshower trickles
Of hope glisten
'Gainst glass;
I raise my cup:
This too shall pass!
Feed the ground
With spirit-kisses;
Bless me with
Your wise whispers
Of Green Lore
And Dyr-Andar secrets.
Land, sea, and air,
I call upon the Landvaettir:
Stand with me;
Stand beside.
Soar above;
In peace reside.

MARCH 9

I call down the rain
And sing:
Laguz Laguz Thurisaz
Thurisaz Laguz
Isa Nauthiz Laguz
Laguz Thurisaz
Thurisaz Laguz.
I sprinkle here
An offering for
Sprinkles in return:
Gift for gift,
With gratitude.
Hail Thor,
Farmer's Friend;
God That Brings The Rain.
I sing for You:
Laguz Laguz Thurisaz
Thurisaz Laguz
Isa Nauthiz Laguz
Laguz Thurisaz
Thurisaz Laguz.

MARCH 10

Sprout grow;
Tree bud:
I call upon the Green Wights;
You souls of leaf and twig.
I thank you
For the blessings
To come,
And for blessings
That have been.
I pour for you water,
Sweet and clear;
I warm the earth
With hands and breath,
To welcome you here.
I call upon the Green Wights;
You souls of flower and vine.
I pray for you to waken,
And feel the sun again.
Grow strong;
Grow tall;
Grow beautiful.
I call upon the GreenWights;
You souls of grass and bark.
For you I pour out
Brightest blessings,
Where seeds dwell
In the comforting dark.
Sprout grow;
Tree bud.

MARCH 11

Dyr-andi, dyr-andi, dyr-andi:
I wait patiently;
Please come close to me.
Let me know you;
Come to guard and guide.
Let me dance with you;
Move with you;
Learn to move *like* you.
Sit with me,
Beneath the Great Tree,
In shadow of Yggdrasil.
Speak to me and through me
And with me, to soothe me.
I offer up my heart's kindness;
My mind's open door.
Dyr-andi, dyr-andi, dyr-andi:
I wait patiently;
Please come close to me.
Let me know you;
Come to guard and guide.

MARCH 12

By your Hallowed Names,
I charge this rune:
Nauthiz.
Sigyn's Rune;
Need-Rune;
Rune of resistance leading to strength.
Sign of delays and restrictions;
Of endurance, survival, determination, self-
  reliance, and the will to overcome.
I carve you thus;
With your help, I advise against deprivation,
  imprisonment, and distress.
I paint you the black and blue of bruises hard-won;
I prove you through standing fast in the face of
  trials; through innovation born of strength of will.
I pray you: *Overcome.*
I blot you via personal acts of endurance and
  determination.
I send you forth as strength and compassionate
  endurance for myself;
Strength and compassionate endurance for those I
  hold dear.

MARCH 13

I am needful
As the rising sap
In trees
Reaching for Sunna's face
And wanting to touch.
I am needful
As deer who thirst
In the wilderness,
Standing by streams
Strewn with stones.
I am needful
As stone for earth,
As water for flowing.
Come to me,
Fairest Freyr!
Come again,
Reawaken!
Come up from
Mound
And down from
Stair.
Grace me with
Your Light,
Ingvi-Freyr:
I am needful
As the rising sap
In trees.

MARCH 14

Electric life
Coursing through veins
As horses,
Hooves pounding,
Against ocean waves:
Ing!
Rising Inguz,
Rune of oak;
Acorn-shaped
And quickening.
Quicken me:
Fire to flame to fire;
Fire to flame to flower!
Sap rise;
Sunrise;
Green-wise,
Made new.
Electric life:
Seed the new day.
Ing!
Rising Inguz,
Rune of oak;
Acorn-shaped
And quickening,
Quicken me!

MARCH 15

Ratatosk
Scurry up that Tree
Ratatosk
Tell the Truth to me
I can handle it
I can handle it
Ratatosk
Whisper secrets
Of Hugr and Hamingja
Ratatosk
Whisper secrets
Of balance
That will set me free
I can handle it
I can handle it
Ratatosk

MARCH 16

By your Hallowed Names,
I charge this rune:
Uruz.
Thrudh's Rune;
Aurochs-Rune;
Rune of the strength of mountains;
Of energy and strength;
Of courage and potent action.
I carve you thus;
With your help, I advise against weakness, sickness,
    obsession, domination, and violence.
I paint you green and brown cow-colors;
I prove you through being strong and hale and free
    and wise.
I pray you: *Understand.*
I blot you with meat and physical action.
I send you forth as strength and good health for
    myself;
Strength and good health for those I hold dear.

MARCH 17

Make me green again:
Paint me
Growing colors
That strain against
Stagnation.
Unbind me
From the status quo;
Make me wild
Enough
To take right-chances;
Wise enough
To know the difference.
Holy Freyr,
Bright Freyr:
Caress me as the bright,
Young buds of trees;
The swaying sprouts
Of new-grown wheat.
I offer this light to You,
To mirror Your own;
Pour sweet fruits of vine
And tree for You,
To quench Your
Aching thirst.
Make me green again.

SIGRBLOT

MARCH 18

Nights full nine
I pour and offer:
A third at summer;
That was Sigrblot.
At this start of
Summer-season,
This time we
Now call Spring:
Third Great Festival
Of the Wheel.
I blot for Victory:
Let me see
Success
From the seeds
That I have
Planted
In my life.
Let me have
Good seasons.
I blot for Peace:
Let me find
Comfort
In my time of need;
Solace
In the successes
I have sown.

--Portions from *Ynglingasaga*, translation mine.

SIGRBLOT

MARCH 19

Thanks I give
For the victories
Of this year,
And for the victories
Yet to come:
I sing Fehu
For wealth
New-gained;
Jera
For wealth
Maintained.
I sing Kenaz
For those things made
Manifest;
Wunjo
For happiness.
I sing Berkano
For the ways
In which
I've grown;
Inguz
For self-esteem
New-owned.
Thanks I give
For Victories,
Won and yet to come:
Gift for gift,
This offering
Is done.

SIGRBLOT

MARCH 20

Winter's darkness gives way to
Sunna's lengthening journey.
   Hail the Victory of the Sun!
Warming days heat the earth,
Awakening the seeds within.
   Hail the Victory of the Sun!
Freyr visits and Thor blesses the fields
As the sprouts emerge from their slumber.
   Hail the Victory of the Sun!
Ostara brings the turning time
To welcome the change and gladden our hearts.
   Hail the Victory of the Sun!
She shimmers with the colors of the flowers
Reaching for the sun.
   Hail the Victory of the Sun!
Honor Her this tide with colored eggs,
With beautiful songs and bright remembrances.
   Hail the Victory of the Sun!
Hail to Ostara, Goddess of the Spring--
Renewing our hearts with love, hope, and joy!
   Hail the Victory of the Sun!

--Italicized portions by Jan Tjeerd,
Gifts of the Wyrd

SIGRBLOT

MARCH 21

Hail Sigyn,
Mother of Compassion!
I hold this bowl
In Your stead;
Though only for the
Briefest of times,
In comparison to
Your forever.
May it serve as
A lesson for me
In compassionate strength,
That I may go
Forward in life
With Your steadfast
And loving heart.
Hail Sigyn,
Victorious!
I hold this bowl
In Your stead;
Though only for the
Briefest of times,
In comparison to
Your forever.
May it serve as
A lesson for me
In endurance,
That I may strive
Harder in life
To meet my goals.
Enda er, ok enda skal vera.
Blessed be.

SIGRBLOT

MARCH 22

Galdr-Goddess,
Teach me to
Sing:
Sowilo Tiwaz Sowilo.
Victory, health, and
Wholeness;
Cleansing fire!
Sowilo Tiwaz Sowilo.
Honor, Justice, and
Victory!
Sowilo Tiwaz Sowilo.
Victory, health, and
Wholeness;
Cleansing fire!
I sing for Sigyn.
Sowilo Tiwaz Sowilo.
I sing for Sigyn:
Galdr Hapt;
Galdr-Bond,
Incantation-Fetter.
Sing the incantation
As offering:
Sowilo Tiwaz Sowilo.
Hail, Sigyn!
Sowilo Tiwaz Sowilo.
Hail, Sigyn!
Sowilo Tiwaz Sowilo.

--*Galdr Hapt* referenced from *Thorsdrapa*,
translation mine.

SIGRBLOT

MARCH 23

Hail, Sigyn,
Mother Strong;
She Who stands between
Me and my fears:
Hold the cup,
And catch their poison;
Shield my face from their sting.
Teach me not only to endure,
But to rise above.
And when calm washes over me,
And peace again returns,
Let me turn my mind
To thank You,
And my heart toward love.
Blessed be.

SIGRBLOT

MARCH 24

Bound that she lay under Cauldron-Grove,
Guilefully perceived Loki similarly;
There sat Sigyn
Yet not of her husband chose joy.
Would you know yet more—or what?
Hold the basin
O'er the fire,
Oh You of Victorious Galdr!
What the Volva
Guilefully beheld,
Let us come to finally
Understand:
Offerings given to flame.
Would you know yet more—or what?
Cauldron-Grove
I build for you:
Candles all a-glow;
Cups that catch,
And bowls that sing.
Would you know yet more—or what?
And I would!
Incense reek this space;
Make it clean.
I call down
Victory:
Hail, Sigyn Loki's-Wife!
Less the burden of His arms,
Than He of Yours.
Hail!

--Portions from *Voluspa* 35, translation mine

SIGRBLOT

MARCH 25

There is
Another way forward
Show me
Another way forward
Sigrblot:
Another way forward
Blot for successful summer raids;
Another way forward
Yet, we no longer go on summer raids!
Another way forward
Or do we?
Another way forward
Likely also to bless newly-planted crops;
Another way forward
Many of us no longer plant crops.
Another way forward
Or do we?
Another way forward
We all seek new horizons;
Another way forward
All set future goals;
Another way forward
All plant seeds of hope,
Another way forward
And of things hoped for:
Another way forward
These are now our "summer raids";
Another way forward
Our "newly planted crops".
Another way forward
I pray for
Another way forward.

SIGRBLOT

MARCH 26

Early shall rise,
He who otherwise wild
Assets or vitality would have;
Seldom the lying-down wolf
Gets the thigh
Nor the sleeping man victory.
Therefore,
Let me be awake!
Awake:
To my own needs,
And the needs of the many;
My own justice,
And justice-in-community.
Awake:
To my Gods' voices,
As well as my own;
To the goals I set for myself,
As well as the goals set for me.
Allfather,
Help me rise early
To the challenges
In my life.
Sigyn,
Teach me to endure
So that I do not fall
Asleep.
For I would have
The gift of Fehu:
Wealth and vitality that move,
Yet not *away* from me.
--Portions from *Havamal* 58, translation mine.

SIGRBLOT

MARCH 27

Let me be called
Dreamchaser,
Peacespeaker,
Justiceholder,
Goalsetter;
Victorious!
Let this last offering
Of Sigrblot
Be not my last offering
Given,
But a pouring out--
First, and last, and always--
Of gifts for all of the gifts
Made manifest in my life.
I pour for Sigyn,
Who holds the cup;
I pour for Loki,
Who is the fire-offering
Of hogr, and ve, and stalli-shelf.
I pour for Odin,
Who teaches me;
I pour for Freyr,
Who invigorates.
Let me be revived,
And taught;
Let me set Worlds ablaze
With my shouts of
Victory.

MARCH 28

I rise,
Blue sky blinding,
To meet this day,
And the coming days,
Knowing I am made anew.
Sloughing off winter's chill,
As the world sloughs off snow,
I am made anew.
In no one's likeness
But my own,
I fare me forth:
Not only to Otherworlds,
But in this mundane one as well,
For I am made anew.
So much have I learned,
Within the labyrinth
Of Winter's dark:
Fire, sealed within Ice;
Ice, quenched by Fire.
The cup puts out the candle;
Water raises seeds.
I am made anew.
I am grateful, and
I rise.

MARCH 29

Troubled is as troubled does,
And I shall not be
Troubled.
No more wallowing,
As pigs in mud.
If I have learned anything,
It is this:
The unwise man is awake all night,
And thinks of anything-whatever;
There is mourning, moodiness, and exhaustion
   when morning comes,
And all the wretchedness is the same as it was.
Worry changes nothing,
Nor does wallowing.
Common sense protects people,
Never seek to obtain too much wisdom:
The past avenges itself on us with knowledge
   beforehand;
No one knows their fate,
And that frees us from a sorrowful mind.
Praise Freyr and Thor
For common sense!
I refuse to always look backwards,
Over my shoulder,
Into the past:
I am not going that way.

--Portions from *Havamal* 23 and 56,
translation mine

MARCH 30

Parts of me are broken,
And parts of me are whole;
Parts of me still question,
And parts of me just *know*.
A sword is more than the gemstones,
Encrusted on its hilt;
I am more than some epitaph
Of brokenness and guilt.
Legacies live in me:
Of Ancestors into whose line I'm born,
And Ancestors of Path and Kith.
Such is the balance
Of Hugr and Hamingja:
It is a form of careful
Smithcraft.
We must endure the fire,
To be remade.
I pour this blot
For Volundr,
Greatest of the Smiths:
Help me forge my balance.
Legacies live in me:
Of Ancestors into whose line I'm born,
And Ancestors of Path and Kith.
Parts of me just *know* things,
And parts of me still question;
Parts of me are whole;
Parts of me still broken.
But a fire has been lit in me,
And I burn.

MARCH 31

I let go of the past,
To find my future.
I embraced Death,
To understand my life.
"Life is for the living"
Does not mean
What too many people
Think it means:
It means, instead, to honestly *live*!
Sometimes the Dead
Come to love us,
And likewise to be loved.
That does not mean
That Life is not for them:
It means that *living*
Is for all of us to *do*.
Everything happens
In the space
Between:
Life is for the living.
Let me go forth,
And *live*!

APRIL 1

There is the trick of it:
To laugh,
And have the laugh
Not be a lie.
To celebrate
The pure and honest
Joy of things,
Even when the clouds loom,
And the rains come;
Gift me that,
As I now gift You.
Hail, Loki,
Master of Change;
Sage of the Misfits
And the Broken:
Bless me with
Courage
To laugh at myself,
Even as I learn
From my own mistakes.
Teach me the lessons
Of the Divine Fool:
That to truly land
Where we belong,
Sometimes we must
Take that first step
Off of the perceived cliff,
Laughing,
All the way down....

APRIL 2

Into
Every life
A little rain
Must fall:
Let each drop
Kiss
My face,
As a hallow.
Bless me,
Thor,
That I may
Hearken
To plainly
Spoken words:
Simplicity breeds
Wisdom.
Bless me,
Heimdall,
For we are
Kin:
I give thanks
For my
Ancestors.
Rain, fall;
Drops, kiss:
Let me be
Hallowed.
Let me be
Blessed.

APRIL 3

Birds fly back;
Memory,
On wings.
Swans
Settle on lakes
Of glass,
Fresh-thawed
Harbors
Of springtimes-past.
Return,
Return!
Fly back,
And remember;
Bind back
And surrender:
To Hamingja-bound,
And Hugr-balanced;
Crying Swan-maids
Who rise
As Valkyries
And as Disir.
Help me
Don those same wings
And likewise
Rise.

APRIL 4

Still waters
Run deep:
Let me be
Still.
Help me be
Still.
Slow my breath
To the drum
Of the Earth's
Heartbeat,
That I may
Hear
What Spring
Has to say
To me.
Reach my roots
Deep
Into this ground
On which
I sit,
For I am
Of the Earth,
And Earth
Is of me.
Still waters
Run deep:
Let me be
Still.

APRIL 5

Carry me down
To the Golden Wood,
At orchard verge,
By a low wall of stone,
Where Idunna fosters
The first seeds
Of what will be again,
Come autumn.
Carry me down
To keep company
With Bragi's bride,
And pass the time
Slowly.
Carry me down
To that place
Where East meets West,
And Between becomes
Manifest.
Carry me down
And let me
Tarry there,
To learn and
To know and
To will and
To be wise.
Carry me down.

APRIL 6

Blessed Day!
Blessed Daeg!
Rise to meet us,
As we rise to meet!
Let me greet
The sunrise
With hope
And gratitude;
With promise,
And the knowing
That even
Promises
Unfulfilled
Hold unsuspected
Blessings.
Bless the Day!
Bless Fair Daeg!
A kiss,
From my lips,
Held to the sky:
Blessed Day!
Blessed Daeg!
Skinfaxi ride swift;
Mane blazing,
To light our way.

APRIL 7

Sunna,
Sun-faced,
Shine!
May our gratitude
For each day
Be swift and bright--
Bright as Your journey
Across the sky.
Sunwise and
Radiant,
Kiss our skin with light,
That we may hold its hope
In our memory,
Even in the darkest night.
Sunna,
Sun-faced,
Shine!
May our hope
In this new day
Be renewed,
Promises be kept;
Goals pursued.
Sunna,
Sun-faced,
Shine!

APRIL 8

Thorn and thistle grow
In hedgerow and in dale;
Vines reach and hallow
Spaces in between.
Huldrafolk dance beneath
Shadowed moonglow,
Calling me to join
In trolldomr secret;
Trolldomr that enchants.
Come, let me join
Hiddenfolk and Eld;
Troll and Nisse and Tomte,
Glaistig, Gnome, and Alf.
Come, let me join!
Come, let me join!
Steps and leaps in hedgerow;
Twirls and swoons in dale:
Come, then, let me join!
Thorn and thistle grow;
Strike drum and sound the horn:
Let me dance with
Hiddenfolk and Eld;
Troll and Nisse and Tomte,
Glaistig, Gnome, and Alf!

APRIL 9

Hands I have
For gifting;
Hands I have
To bless:
Praise the Gods
For these hands
Of mine,
Let them work
Toward Justice;
Let them bring
Forth light.
Hands I have
For gifting;
Hands I have
To bless;
Praise the Gods
For these hands
Of mine:
Let them
Not be idle;
Let them work
For Good.

APRIL 10

Dagaz
I sing the bright new day;
Dagaz
I sing my liberation!
Dagaz
I sing for hope relaimed;
Dagaz
I sing with jubilation!
Dagaz
I sing for life new-born;
Dagaz
I sing at daybreak,
To thank the burning morn!
Dagaz
I sing the bright new day;
Dagaz
I sing my liberation!
Dagaz
I sing for hope relaimed;
Dagaz
I sing with jubilation!

APRIL 11

Fire burn,
And flame kindle;
Wheel turn
As Wyrd's spindle:
Manifest the flaxen thread
Of destiny achieved,
Of goals accomplished
Once set.
Fire burn,
And flame kindle;
Wheel turn
As Wyrd's spindle:
Restore balance
As embers glow
A radiant borealis:
Northern fire
Within my soul,
Many-colored-bright.
Fire burn,
And flame kindle:
Brand kindles brand,
Until it burns with flames,
Flame is kindled from fire;
Wheel turn
As Wyrd's spindle:
Fire burn in me.

--Portions from *Havamal* 57, translation mine.

APRIL 12

As the oak reaches for the sun,
I reach for You:
I raise my voice as birdsong,
Calling, calling,
Calling You home.
Come and be kind;
Come and stay awhile.
Rest Your hands
Upon my shoulders
In frithful embrace.
Come and be kind;
Come and stay awhile.
Come and take these gifts
I bring, and exchange them
For blessings.
As the oak reaches for the sun,
I reach for You:
Beloved Aesir,
Sweet Gods, and Wise;
As the birds sing,
I raise my voice for You:
Blessed Vanir,
Sweet Gods, and Wise.
Come and be kind;
Come and stay awhile.
Rest Your hands
Upon my shoulders
In frithful embrace.

APRIL 13

Let there ever be
Peace between us;
Good seasons shared
In bountiful blot.
Let there ever be
Love between us;
Hearts raised in praise
And gratitude.
Let there ever be
Space on my altar
For work to be done;
Time in my morning
For prayers to be sung.
Let there ever be
Peace between us;
Good seasons shared
In bountiful blot.
Let there ever be
Love between us;
Hearts raised in praise
And gratitude.
Let there ever be
Frith between us;
Let what is paid
Be repaid in turn,
Gift for gift;
Song for song.

APRIL 14

Gerdha,
In this fruitful season,
Remind me to
Pause:
To stop a moment,
At my garden gate,
And admire the
Flowers
Growing there;
To soak in the sun,
As it falls through my
Window.
Let me take
Those extra moments
To listen to sweet
Birdsong;
To offer up a prayer
Of thanks
For all those things
Given
To me in my life,
By the Gods,
And by others.
Help me remember
That the sweetest
Blessings
Are those we never
Asked for,
But were given to us
Anyway.

APRIL 15

Grace
Is a gift
That is given to us,
Even when
Unasked;
Even when
Undeserved.
We do nothing
To earn it,
Save being.
It is not
A purely
Christian thing,
Though many
Certainly claim it
As a thing
All their own.
No--
It is in
Each drop of rain;
Every roadside flower;
Every passing second
Spent within
Every passing hour.
Every breath
We have not
Asked to breathe
Is a gift of
Grace.

APRIL 16

Good green Earth
Made up of
Good dark earth:
I pour the simplest
Of libations
Upon the bosom of Jord.
Water,
Fresh and clear,
For seed and sprout
Which foster here;
For thirsty squirrel
And bird on wing;
For Landvaettir,
This drink I bring.
I bring to bless,
And blessed I bring:
Water,
Sweet and fresh and clear,
For good green Earth
Of good dark earth,
And all those
Who would linger here.

APRIL 17

Branch of birch
For Frigga's grace;
Smiling daffodil
To mirror Sunna's face.
Roses, vined and reaching,
Reflect the passion
Of Freyja's teachings.
Purple pansies
For the Aesir;
Odin, Allfather,
Smile on me.
As my garden grows,
So, too, faith and practice;
Into each sprig and leaf,
The Gods weave Their own magick.
Landvaettir on silent feet
Tread even now
Through my humble yard,
And I do my utmost
To maintain the frith
That keeps them innangard.

APRIL 18

Time outside of time I find
In Place outside of place;
Bless me now as I weave this hallow
O'er this Sacred Space.
Gods enshrined by rhymes entwined
Embrace and are embraced;
Bless me now as I weave this hallow
To mark this Sacred Space.
Jormungandr's dancer I've become,
Encircling as the Serpent what's begun:
Bless me now, as hallow-weaver ,
The maker and the made;
Bless me now as I weave this hallow
Around this Sacred Space.
Time outside of time I find
In Place outside of place....

APRIL 19

Memory goes to ground
In springtime,
In favor of the new.
We cease to work within,
Releasing ourselves
From our hibernation.
We slough off
Outmoded skins;
Ways of doing things.
But there are yet
Things unforgettable:
The smile of a brother;
The laugh of a sister;
The touch of a mother;
The scent of a lover.
Memory goes to ground
In springtime,
In favor of the new.
Yet memory ever lingers
Of those times and ones
That are Tru.

APRIL 20

At the base of
The Spiral Stair
I stand in good faith:
Oathsworn and Honor-bound.
Help me climb
To Alfheim,
In Salarsalur
To dwell.
Let me learn
The secrets
Of those long
Gone before;
Tales of Ancestors
Of Kith and Kin;
Of Blood and Bone;
Of Path and Skin.
Show me the
Old Ways,
That I may
Birth them
New.
And in all
I learn
And all
I teach,
Keep me
Ever-tru.

APRIL 21

Salarsular:
Hall of Halls,
Gleaming bright;
Pride of Alfheim's
Glistening height.
Lintels carved
Of honored words,
Hewn in gold
Of oaths fair-sworn
Are there;
A doorway to
Ancestral Wisdom
Within.
There let me tarry;
Let me carry forth
From those
Hallowed halls
Some of what
Was known
And unknown
In the great
Before.

APRIL 22

Hail, Freyr,
Light-Bringer;
Lord of Mound
And Height;
Tooth-bound
King of Alfheim,
Hail, and Well-met!
Hail, likewise,
Winged Wayland,
Volundr the Smith
Who is called
Visi-Alfa,
Hail, and Well-met!
You princes of Alfheim;
Lords of the Air
And of Light:
Kindle my world
With Craft,
And with Inspiration;
Teach me to
Work for what
I love,
And to love
What is wrought.
On this Spring Eve,
I pour for You:
Heart ready;
Mind open.

APRIL 23

Dust upon the curtains,
Webs upon the sill:
Spring cleaning is such a chore,
Yet clean this house I will!
Bless it, please,
Good Husvaettir,
With your presence
Everywhere:
In the corners of my kitchen:
By doorway, stoop, and stair.
And if you'd kindly join me
In my sweeping of its rooms,
There's milk for you, and cookies,
And space upon my broom.
Dust upon the curtains,
Webs upon the sill:
Spring cleaning is such a chore,
Yet clean this house I will!

April 24

Sweet Sif,
Bless this house
With frith:
Let no trouble come
To my door.
Fair Frigga,
Bless this house
With hygge:
Let my family know
Only comfort and warmth.
Gentle Gerdha,
Bless this house
With hope:
Let us not
Await in vain.
Kiss the lintels
Of my doorway
With protective light,
And each friend
Who enters 'neath them
With hospitality's rite.
Enda er, ok enda skal vera.

APRIL 25

Laguz Ansuz Mannaz
Laguz Ansuz Ing!
A healing song,
A healing song,
A healing song I sing!
Laguz Ansuz Mannaz
Laguz Ansuz Ing!
Galdr fair for ears of Eir,
I raise in offering!
Laguz Ansuz Mannaz
Laguz Ansuz Ing!
A healing song,
A healing song,
A healing song I sing!
Laguz Ansuz Mannaz
Laguz Ansuz Ing!
Pain eclipse;
Soothe suffering!
Laguz Ansuz Mannaz
Laguz Ansuz Ing!
A healing song,
A healing song,
A healing song I sing!
Laguz Ansuz Mannaz
Laguz Ansuz Ing!
Wound and disease be gone;
Renewed health and haleness bring!
Laguz Ansuz Mannaz
Laguz Ansuz Ing!

APRIL 26

I draw three tines
Upon my door:
Algiz, to protect.
Baldur's rune,
Elk-rune,
Rune of shield and victor.
I draw three tines
Upon my door:
Algiz, to give shelter.
Baldur's rune,
Elk-rune,
Rune of God-connections.
I draw three tines
Upon my door:
Algiz, to defend.
Baldur's rune,
Elk-rune,
Rune of divine deflection.
Protect and guard:
My home,
My life,
The ones I love,
From hidden dangers,
Broken swears,
Oaths denied,
And Gods-forgotten.
Enda er, ok enda skal vera.

APRIL 27

Fair travels and bright horizons
For myself;
Fair travels and bright horizons
For all those I hold dear.
Let me be moved:
Let me never gather dust,
Unless it be that dust
Of long roadways,
Pleasantly travelled.
Let them be moved likewise:
Let them never know
Stagnation's pain,
Nor feel that they have
Toiled in vain.
I look to the South:
To Hela's dark doorway.
Lady Death,
Remind us how to
Live.
Fair travels and bright horizons
For myself;
Fair travels and bright horizons
For all those I hold dear.

APRIL 28

Stand me by a riverside,
Else by lake or stream;
Set my feet on sandy beach,
By ocean's ebbing tide.
Let me pour a blot for You,
Lord Noatan;
Van-Father Njordr.
In peace, I make this offering:
I set it afloat;
Onward to new horizons,
As I myself would go.
Let it neither sink
Nor be still;
Let me neither sink
Nor be still.
Instead:
Flow.
Cleanse.
Create.
Heal.

APRIL 29

Freyr Njordrsson,
Bright Brother
Of The Lady:
Great Vanic Lord,
Hear me now;
Be near me now.
Set a hand upon
My shoulder,
That I may know
I am not alone.
Restore to me
The self-esteem
I knew once,
Perhaps too long ago.
Remind me
I am worthy,
As does Your Sister, dear.
Restore to me
Your blessings,
As I pour this offering here.

APRIL 30

Walpurgisnacht
They call it now;
Its old name,
Long forgot.
Hexennacht
Was banished
By the Abbess,
Yet we now
Reclaim this season
For the Vanir
And their patrons,
Who under Christians
Became "witches".
I celebrate the Seidhrkona
Upon her gilded chair;
The Volva, her distaff raised,
Ready to wield and weave Wyrd.
I celebrate the Vitki
Who sings high and proud;
Let him reveal the runes again,
And lift from them their shroud.
All you brave
Norse Witches,
Reclaim what was forgot:
Dance again and lift the veil
To reclaim
Hexennacht!

VANIRBLOT

MAY 1

I sing for Freyr's Messenger,
Skirnir:
Ansuz Ansuz Ansuz.
I sing for the Lovers,
Odh and Gerdh:
Gebo Wunjo Gebo.
I sing for the Mother,
Nerthus:
Othala.
I sing for the Warrior,
Freyr with antler raised:
Algiz Inguz Algiz.
I sing for Njordr,
Sage of Peace:
Laguz Laguz Jera.
And I sing for The Lady:
Perdhro Fehu Kenaz
Kenaz Fehu Perdhro
Kenaz.
Let there ever be peace
Between me and Thee,
And good seasons in my life,
And in the lives of those
That I hold dear.

VANIRBLOT

MAY 2

You call,
And I come to you;
I dream,
And You are there:
Red-Gold Woman
Of ecstatic tears,
You chase my fears
Away
And teach me
To see
Inside myself.
Hail Freyja!
I call,
And You come to me;
I dream,
And You are there:
Fruitful Learned Man*
Of mound and field,
You increase my yield
In all ways
And teach me
To see
Inside myself.
Hail Freyr!

*Frode, Frothi, Frodhi are all suggested as by-names of Freyr; traditionally translated as "burgeoning" or "fruitful", these words are more properly translated as "knowing magick, charms, or spells"

VANIRBLOT

MAY 3

Ask me to pour for You;
Ask me to kneel.
Ask me to sing to You;
Ask me to heal.
Ask me to draw runes
Upon my arms
And hammers in the sky.
Ask me to hallow;
Ask me to cry.
Ask me to bury
Secrets in the sand;
To honor the Ancestors,
My fellow Humans;
The Land.
Ask and I'll give You,
Yet ask me not this:
Please never ask me
My Gods to forget.
I'll pour til I'm empty;
I'll kneel til I'm tired.
I'll sing til my voice breaks;
I'll heal what's inside.
I'll draw runes
On my arms, no matter who judges;
Throw hammer-sign to hallow
Without apology.
I'll set apart sacred space;
I'll never hide my tear-stained face.
Others need never understand
Why I honor my Ancestors,
My Gods and the Land;
My fellow Humans:

Each Woman and Man.
My faith is my everything:
My Gods are my shield.
And no one can take from me
The Power They yield:
The Love and the Wisdom,
The Trust and the Troth.
I am fulltrui of One,
Yet bound to the lot.
Ask me to pour for You;
Ask me to kneel.
Ask me to sing to You;
Ask me to heal.
Ask me to draw runes
Upon my arms
And hammers in the sky.
Ask me to hallow;
Ask me to cry.
Ask me to bury
Secrets in the sand;
To honor the Ancestors,
My fellow Humans;
The Land.
Ask and I'll give You,
Yet ask me not this:
Please never ask me
My Gods to forget.

MAY 4

I stand at the cusp
Of Darkness and Light,
Seeking ever
A balance to find.
Lord of the Mound
Who is
Lord of Alfheim,
Help me the
Spiral Stairway to climb.
Show me the midpoint
Between Life and Death,
And teach me that Living
Means doing my best.
Guide me towards Passion
That promotes only Peace;
Help me tame my emotions
To find serenity.
Show me the order
Within the chaos;
Make of me a Justice-wielder
Who restores the balance.
Hail Holy Frodhi:
Fruitful in Knowledge!
I offer this gift to Thee,
In solemn homage.
I stand at the cusp
Of Darkness and Light,
Seeking ever
A balance to find.

MAY 5

By your Hallowed Names,
I charge this rune:
Kenaz.
Freyja's Rune;
Torch-Rune;
Rune of vision and creativity.
Sign of knowledge and inspiration;
Of the fire of life, regeneration, and transformation.
I carve you thus;
With your help, I advise against apathy, instability,
    disease, and false hope.
I paint you the red of passion;
I prove you by being passionately creative; by
    creating my own reality and accepting and
    understanding my own power.
I pray you: *Manifest*.
I blot you with fire and incense and artistry.
I send you forth as creativity and the manifestation
    of hoped-for dreams for myself;
Creativity and the manifestation of hoped-for
    dreams for those I hold dear.

MAY 6

Kindle the flame of Will:
Heilag-Vilja,
To make magick
And move storms.
Skjalf,
Set me to shake;
To tremble with
Heilag-Vilja:
The Holy Will
That sparks
And ignites.
Holy Freyja,
Odin's Third Teacher:
Teach me,
Likewise.
Set me alight
With the fire
Of Kenaz!
Make of me
A Wyrd-Weaver;
Wyrd-Shaper;
Wyrd-Seer,
As the Sacred Norns.
Kindle the flame of Will:
Heilag-Vilja,
To make magick
And move storms.

MAY 7

Gefn
Gift me
Wisdom;
Skjalf
Set me
Ablaze:
Heilag-Vilja
Fill me,
To wield
And bring forth
Change.
Valfreyja
Guide my
Choices;
Syr
Bestow
Rebirth:
Grant that
I should
Wield
Your Power
Upon this
Middle-Earth.
Enda er, ok enda skal vera.
Enda er, ok enda skal vera.
Enda er, ok enda skal vera.

MAY 8

Fire crackle;
Flame pop,
Before the shadowed glass.
Raudh-Gull
Fuel my passion;
Teach me how to dance.
Let me move to the rhythm
Of my beaten drum;
Raise the energy of
Gifted Will given by Gefn.
Heilag-Vilja fill my magick;
Heilag-Vilja shape my Wyrd.
Heilag-Vilja fuel my ecstasy
As I work with the Vanir.
Vanadis
I pray You'll hear me:
Teach me how to dance.
Gift me with clear-vision
As I move through this trance.
Fire crackle;
Flame pop:
Will fire this work!
Heilag-Vilja fill my magick;
Heilag-Vilja shape my Wyrd.
Heilag-Vilja fuel my ecstasy
As I work with the Vanir.

MAY 9

By your Hallowed Names,
I charge this rune:
Inguz.
Ingvi-Freyr's Rune;
Earth-Rune;
Rune of common sense and simple strength.
Sign of masculine virility and familial warmth;
Of rest, relief, and freedom.
I carve you thus;
With your help, I advise against impotence,
   stagnation, and toil.
I paint you the green and brown of the growing oak;
I prove you each time I listen to myself and use
   common sense; each time I practice self-care;
   each time I show familial warmth to another
   being.
I pray you: *Free Me.*
I blot you with acorn and oak branch; with warm,
   fertile earth.
I send you forth as warmth, love, and freedom for
   myself;
Warmth, love, and freedom for those I hold dear.

MAY 10

Innovation breeds
Transformation breeds
Regeneration to
Free me from
Stagnation.
Isa Tiwaz Raidho
Ing!
Kenaz Jera Wunjo
Ing!
Mighty galdr now I sing;
Pouring every
Ounce of Will
Into this offering.
Freyja to fill me;
Freyr to heal,
And teach me
Every drop of skill
That might be
Learned in
Alfheim's heights,
Or gained
By Fjadhrhamr-flight!
For change and rebirth,
Now I sing:
Isa Tiwaz Raidho
Ing!
Kenaz Jera Wunjo
Ing!

MAY 11

Empower me
To love
The person
That I am;
Empower me
To change
The world
In which I live.
Empower me
To know
My limits
And my strengths;
Empower me
To will
Myself to
Go to greater lengths.
Empower me
To dream
When others say
All hope is lost;
Empower me
To believe
No matter how great
The cost.

MAY 12

Born and reborn
Through fire and pyre;
Through tests and trials,
As Gullveig's Power.
I am the raven on the wing;
I am the wind beneath.
I am the notes of runes wise-sung;
I am the voice that sings.
Teach me to burn
With vibrant Will;
To ever-reach for change.
Teach me to know
Myself;
My Gods,
To better meet life's tests.
Kindle my heart
To burn as
Heidhr:
A bright and shining witch.
I am the raven on the wing;
I am the wind beneath.

MAY 13

Move together;
Move apart.
Turn loving You
Into Loving Art.
Pour myself out
And deep into;
Pour myself out
To be birthed anew.
Into out of inside within;
Breath to breath;
Skin on skin.
Move together;
Move apart.
Turn loving You
Into Loving Art.
Sex and Death
And Ecstasy,
Woven together
Inside of me.
Pour myself out
And deep into;
Pour myself out
To be birthed anew.

MAY 14

I meet you halfway;
That's what love means.
I meet my Gods halfway;
That's what love means.
Give and take;
Gift for gift.
That's how love speaks;
That's what it does.
Because,
Not despite;
No excuses.
That's how love
Understands.
My hand in your hand;
Lips to lips to speak,
Words dripping pure
And sweet and true.
I meet you halfway;
That's what love means.
I meet my Gods halfway;
That's what love means.

MAY 15

Give to take;
Take to give:
Gift for gift
Is how I live.
Every word
I ever speak,
In my moments
When I'm weak:
Give to take;
Take to give:
Gift for gift
Is how I live.
Magick is
As magick does;
We can only change
What is, not was.
Give to take;
Take to give:
Gift for gift
Is how I live.
Let me work
With focus strong;
Let me grow
All my life long.
Give to take;
Take to give:
Gift for gift
Is how I live.

MAY 16

Let me be the one
Who meets the needs
Of stranger and of friend;
The helper and the helped:
Wounds mended;
Wounds yet-to-mend.
Compassion bleed
From open pores;
Compassion breathe
As tides on shores.
In and out;
Give and take:
Gift for gift,
Help me make
The difference.
Keep me strong enough
To do the work
That is the business
Of Humankind.
And when at day's end
I find my rest,
Let me sleep
With peaceful mind.
Let me be the one
Who meets the needs
Of stranger and of friend;
The helper and the helped:
Wounds mended;
Wounds yet-to-mend.

MAY 17

My body moves
As waves of grass:
Slow,
And fluid.
My body moves
As sheaves of wheat:
Tall,
And noble.
My body moves
As sky meets sunlight:
Bright,
And beautiful.
My body moves
And I know
I am awake.
Every fiber reaches
For things seen
And yet unseen;
For Will wrought
On a May Eve
Beneath a grove of trees.
For aching stretch
Of skin-gainst-skin,
Lips sharing breath and love.
My body moves
As Gods speak:
Divine,
Rhythmic dance.

MAY 18

By your Hallowed Names,
I charge this rune:
Perdhro.
Disir-Rune;
Lot-cup-Rune;
Rune of mysteries and hidden things.
Sign of initiations and one's own Wyrd;
Of feminine mysteries met in fellowship and with
    joy.
I carve you thus;
With your help, I advise against addiction,
    stagnation, loneliness, and apathy.
I paint you the red and blue of womankind;
I prove you each time I go within to seek the
    unknown and embrace my feminine side.
I pray you: *Reveal.*
I blot you alongside the Disir, and with fire and
    water and smoke and silence.
I send you forth as a fair Wyrd, with fellowship and
    joy, for myself;
A fair Wyrd, with fellowship and joy, for those I
    hold dear.

MAY 19

Pull back the shroud
Upon the wain;
Unveil what lies
Beneath.
Holy Nerthus,
Sacred Mother;
Wife of Njordr:
Invite me into
Forgotten groves
Lingering in the back
Of my mind;
Reveal me as a ghost,
Trembling
In the rear seat
Of a darkened theater,
Waiting to be rescued.
Remind me what was,
So I will remember
What will be.
Show me Your face,
Charmed Sister-Wife;
Mother of Freyja and Freyr.
Gift me with Your presence;
Show me my own way.

MAY 20

The Dead speak
And want to love us;
The Dead speak
And want to touch:
Through the ages
All our Ancestors
Reach past veils
And times
To teach us much.
Do not shirk
The warm embrace
Of cold hands
Reaching from the earth;
Do not tremble
For fear of what was,
Or yet will be.
Would you know yet more,
Or what?
The Dead speak
And want to love us;
The Dead speak
And want to touch.
Through the ages
All the Lost Ones
Shake away their dust.
I *would* know more,
And what....

MAY 21

Rafdis*
Raudh-Gull
Paint my world
Red-gold with
Joy;
Spark bliss
Inside this
Dead heart,
Now new-alive
With Heilag-Vilja.
Show me
How to be
Happy.
Remind me
Of the simple things:
Peppered tracks
Of ants on glass;
Birds on wing
Singing rune-songs.
Cloak me in feathers:
Peregrine,
Soaring light
Across blue sky.
Rafdis
Raudh-Gull
Paint my world
Red-gold with
Joy.

Rafdis: "Amber-Dis"

MAY 22

Birch peels
Skin feels
As paper;
As bark peeled
Freshly from
A tree.
Open my mind
To new birth;
New growth.
Speak through runes
As wind through trees:
Berkano
Berkano
Berkano
Birch reaches
As hands
As heart:
Towards new Light.

MAY 23

You are stronger
Than you think;
More faithful
Than you believe;
Wiser
Than you know;
Rooted,
But with room to grow.
Dig deep.
Plant your heart
Where your soul is.
Helheim is never far away;
Asgard, but a blink
In eyes as dark
As clouded glass.
You are stronger
Than you think;
More faithful
Than you believe;
Wiser
Than you know;
Rooted deep:
Now,
Grow!

MAY 24

Sea-Bright,
Turn my tears
To jewels;
Glitter them
Across the
Ebbing tides.
Mardoll,
Scatter my woes
As seabirds
Scatter at
Splashing waves.
Heal me:
Mold my pain
Into a storm
Of sacred Will.
Soothe me:
Calm the
Heat of hurt
To forge me
Into something
New again.

MAY 25

Sessrumnir calls me
To hallowed halls
Filled with many seats,
Both High and low.
Let me tarry there,
And yet by streamsides
Where horses run
Through fields
Of high-grown wheat.
Let me be with You,
Bright Lady.
Cradle me in sweet embrace
That is at once
Sister-Mother-Lover.
Hands upon my face,
And stroking my hair.
Let me rest with You there,
Bright Lady.
Breathe the May into my heart,
That even in Winter
I may find the heart of Spring.
Teach me to soar
On wings as deft as falcon's:
Drape me in Fjadhrhamr.
Skin-strong and wholehearted
Let me be.
And let me be with You,
Bright Lady.

May 26

I stir a cauldron black
Fire pitched against those
Who would attack
The Heidhrinn Heart
That claims its place as
Witch.
I stir a cauldron black
And my wand is at the ready,
Galdr tuned to sing
Against those who would
Delay a return to living faith.
I stir a cauldron black
And I chant the runes:
Jera Kenaz Nauthiz
Nauthiz Kenaz Jera.
I stir a cauldron black,
Bristling as a boar:
Burn me thrice
Yet I will rise again;
Three times dead,
Yet three times alive once more!
I stir a cauldron black:
Cauldron becomes Well
Becomes cauldron;
Engine of Wyrd and Will.
I stir a cauldron black.

MAY 27

Need rise
And need burn
Need to will;
Will to yearn.
Heilag-Vilja
Rise to meet
The needs
Of magick's
Searing heat.
Fan the flames
Of Just desire;
Stoke the embers;
Feed the fire.
Need rise
And need burn
Need to will;
Will to yearn.
Heilag-Vilja
Rise in me
To quench
The tide
Of Wyrd's
Turn.
Need rise
And need burn
Need to will;
Will to yearn.

MAY 28

Kindle kenning,
Brand igniting brand
Within my mind;
Heart burning
For a yearned-for
Knowing.
Kindle kenning,
That I may reach
For magick,
Yet not get burned.
Will exercised
Is Will thrice-earned.
Kindle kenning,
Let me dare
The Dark and
Yet the Light;
Stillness gains me
Nothing good:
I will not be silent.
Kindle kenning,
Brand igniting brand
Within my mind;
I take up wand
And rune-stone;
Reach out my hand:
Touch the Divine.

MAY 29

Flow
Easy as water
Towards June;
Towards bright
Midsummer.
Rising heat
Paints a shimmer
On the horizon
Of Mardoll:
Dancing.
I see Her face,
And She
Sees mine.
To know is
To love;
To love,
To know.
Such is the
Flow.

MAY 30

Moonbeams on ocean;
Wind against sky.
I celebrate myself today;
I celebrate I.
I am made worthy
Not purely by my Gods,
But by my own Right actions,
Regardless of the odds.
I keep my word when given;
I don't maintain facades.
When it comes to friends,
My loyalty is a thing of legend
All its own:
Gift for gift til the bitter end,
That's the way I roll.
For the stranger:
Hospitality,
No matter the color of their skin;
Regardless of their faith-base,
Or whether they identify
As Women or as Men.
I don't care who you choose to love,
So long as you love them well.
Trouble the good or weak
Within my sight,
And Justice will prevail!
Moonbeams on ocean;
Wind against sky.
I celebrate myself today:
I celebrate I.

MAY 31

One final pause
Before summer
Rolls across
My life:
One final introspection
Before the heat comes;
Before the waves crash.
I look back one final time
Upon my Season with the ice:
The things that I did learn there;
The worthy-learned advice.
I do not regret the cold, then,
Nor my time spent locked inside.
I lived; I learned;
I am made new and whole.
I have come through
The Labyrinth
To find myself now, outside:
Free to dance in the summer breeze,
My heart and mind opened wide.
So I take this extra moment
Here at the end of May,
To look back upon the Winter
And catalog those days.
For all that I have learned in them,
I am truly blessed.
Come, Summer, come:
I am ready to progress.

JUNE 1

By your Hallowed Names,
I charge this rune:
Gebo.
Sif's Rune;
Gift-Rune;
Rune of gifts-in-balance.
Sign of frith and generosity;
Of right-sacrifice and partnerships.
I carve you thus;
With your help, I advise against greed, loneliness,
    obligation, and over-sacrifice.
I paint you the red of blood-debts and oaths;
I prove you by being generous and upholding frith
    wherever I go.
I pray you: *Give*.
I blot you through heartfelt gifts and right action.
I send you forth as peace and bright blessings for
    myself;
Peace and bright blessings for those I hold dear.

JUNE 2

Let me walk along the shoreline,
Or through the shadowed wood;
Ran and Aegir, reveal Your gifts to me,
Or else the Huldrafolk:
For I wander, looking for a wand.
As it says in the Voluspa
Of Baldur and of Hodhr:
Hoenir shall choose the sacred twig,
And the Sons of Odin
Shall dwell in Vanaheim,
Fetching wood.
Let me likewise fetch:
Hoenir, guide my eye and hand
As I wander far and wide.
For I wander, looking for a wand.
Even in my own yard,
Let me be alert,
For there may be hidden treasures
Thriving in the dirt.
For I wander, looking for a wand.
A wand I seek for mighty spells
And other focused work:
Hoenir, guide my eye and hand
And help me wand discern.
For I wander, looking for a wand.

--Portions from *Voluspa* 63, translation mine.

JUNE 3

Hail Hoenir,
Long-legged Mud King!
Grant me the
Wisdom of Birds:
Make me of keen eye,
And keen mind;
Teach me their language,
That I may speak
With Huldrafolk and Alfar;
With Landvaettir and Dyr-Andar.
Grant me the
Gift of Poetry:
Breath of words,
That I may be eloquent;
Depth of words,
That I be only honest.
Fairness of words,
That I permit others
Sometimes to decide;
Help me reach the balance
Of when to rule
And when to coincide.
Hail Hoenir,
Blot I pour:
Gift for gift
I pray You'll grant me;
I ask nothing more.

JUNE 4

May falls away
To the warm winds
Of June,
And I find myself
Singing a different tune:
Gebo for gifts;
Dagaz for the day;
Algiz to keep
The dark things away.
The veil remains thin,
Between this world and theirs:
The Huldrafolk; the Landvaettir.
Dokkalfar range far and wide,
And trolls lounge lazy
In the gathering night.
Bliss I find in warmer weather;
Joy I claim in each endeavor.
My sails are new-filled
With fresher wind;
And I set a-sail,
No need of ship,
For new journeys
With both Kith and Kin.

JUNE 5

Sunna spark my joy;
Let my heart sing
Sowilo!
Sunna spark my joy;
Every day an offering
Sowilo!
Sunna spark my joy;
The days be long and bright
Sowilo!
Sunna spark my joy;
Day follows even the longest night!
Sowilo!
Sowilo!
Sowilo!
I sing!
Sunna, for the gifts You bring!
Warm my skin and
Warm my heart;
Bright and clear
My Heidhrinn art!
Sunna spark my joy;
Let my heart sing
Sowilo!
Sunna spark my joy;
Every day an offering
Sowilo!

JUNE 6

Summer is almost here:
The world, alive with
Anticipation.
Life force, no longer ebbed,
Flows freely toward
Regeneration.
Make it the same with me:
Heart grow, mind open;
Awaken!
Let it be Summer
Inside my heart!
I shall wear a sunny face;
Dance as bees in sunny space:
Spiraling, gyreing, to and fro;
Drawing down the Sun!
I sing hail to Sunna;
Hail to Daeg!
Hail to Njordr,
Who shows the way
For sailing ships
And the family "vacay"!
Hail to Ran and Aegir, too;
Their Nine Daughters:
Hail to You!
Hail to Hoenir,
Long-legged in the mud!
Hail and well met,
Summer!

JUNE 7

May I shine
As Sunna shines:
A bright, clear
Norse Witch!
Hail Heidhr!
Show me how
To burn;
Kindle
The passionate Will
Of magick!
Shine on!
Let me
Shine on!
I pray to
Shine on!
As Sunna shines:
Bright and clear;
A Norse Witch,
Heidhrinn heart
On fire
For what has been,
But even more
For what's
Yet to come.

JUNE 8

By your Hallowed Names,
I charge this rune:
Dagaz.
Daeg's Rune;
Day-Rune;
Rune of breakthroughs and awakenings.
Sign of daylight clarity; of new enterprises;
Of the power of change directed by one's own will.
I carve you thus;
With your help, I advise against imposed limits and
    hopelessness.
I paint you the golden yellow of a bright summer's
    day;
I prove you each time I reach a balance point; each
    time I channel my will; each time I feel secure
    and happy in the wake of transformation.
I pray you: *Awaken.*
I blot you with honey and beeswax; with apples and
    citrus.
I send you forth as awakenings and clarity for
    myself;
Awakenings and clarity for those I hold dear.

JUNE 9

Day endures,
As I, too,
Would endure:
Night stretched tight
Between two
Closer points
Of sunset and
Of dawn.
Radiant as the day:
That's how I would be.
To dance the
Sacred dance
Of bees,
Calling down
The Sun.
To sing
Bright galdr
As dusk falls,
To hold back
The gathering
Night.
Day endures,
As I, too,
Would endure:
Awake with
Daybright clarity.
Hail to Daeg!
Bright blessings from me;
Bright blessings to me!

JUNE 10

Beeswax and honey
Upon my lips;
Apples and citrus
And sweet rose hips:
These are the
Pleasures of Summer.
I am pleasure, too.
Seashells laid upon the shore;
Birds calling,
Mate to mate.
Billowing sails against the blue:
These are the
Treasures of Summer.
I am treasure, too.
I lay my body on the grass;
Green canopies above me.
Sunna's touch on my face
Is soft and warm and lovely.
These are the
Gifts of Summer.
I am a gift, too.

JUNE 11

Radiant beams
Of heavenly light;
Sunna's embrace:
Warm delight.
Svalinn stand
To guard against
A burning
That is too intense!
Let us work
Together
To protect
What always was,
So that it
Always will be.
We must not
Break through
Sunna's shield,
Lest Her embrace
Come to harm,
Not heal.
Radiant beams
Of heavenly light;
Sunna's embrace:
Warm delight.
Let us raise our faces
To the Sun,
In gratitude and love,
As one.

JUNE 12

I sing a song
For dandelions:
I see wishes
Where others
See only weeds.
The mind
Turns on a dime:
One moment,
One thing;
The next,
Another.
Let those thoughts
Chime clear:
Bright and positive
As yellow faces
Turned toward
The Sun.
Let me not
Sow weeds.
Make me light
Of mind:
Thoughts like
Wishes on the wind.
I sing a song
For dandelions:
I see wishes
Where others
See only weeds.

JUNE 13

By your Hallowed Names,
I charge this rune:
Algiz.
Baldur's Rune;
Elk-Rune;
Rune of protection and the warrior spirit.
Shield-sign; sign of shelter and guardianship;
Of awakenings, God-connections, and divine
    instinct.
I carve you thus;
With your help, I advise against hidden danger,
    breaking taboos, and turning away from the
    Gods.
I paint you the red, black, and purple of a warrior's
    shield;
I prove you each time I protect myself and those I
    love; each time I defend against Evil, and hold
    fast to my oaths to my Gods, for They are my
    shield.
I pray you: *Protect*.
I blot you each time I blot my Gods.
I send you forth as protection and connection to
    Gods for myself;
Protection and connection to Gods for those I hold
    dear.

JUNE 14

Clouds gather;
Storm quakes.
Thunder booms;
House shakes.
Lightning strikes;
Winds blow.
Galdr sing:
Sowilo
Isa Isa Laguz
Sowilo!
Children fear;
Dogs bark.
Rain pours down
Too hard.
Waters rise;
Floods flow.
Galdr sing:
Sowilo
Isa Isa Laguz
Sowilo!
Clouds gather;
Storm quakes.
Thunder booms;
House shakes.
Lightning strikes;
Winds blow.
Galdr sing:
Sowilo
Isa Isa Laguz
Sowilo!

JUNE 15

If I could harness
But a glimmer
Of the power
Of the storm,
I believe that
I would shimmer
With energy
Newborn.
I raise my hands
Inside my house,
And open myself up
To the might of Thor,
And the peace of Njordr.
Rain down;
Rain down:
Within,
Upon,
Inside.
Rain down;
Rain down!
Let there be peace
Between Thee and me;
Restore good seasons
To myself, my friends, my family.
Let me borrow
What is given;
Let me give
That I may bless.
Enda er, ok enda skal vera.

JUNE 16

Rolling tides upon the sand
And I seek Lord Noatan:
Freyr's Father, Njordr,
Oh Holy Van,
Be near me now,
And hold my hand.
Help me find the peace in this,
Where it seems now
That no peace lives.
Show to me a brighter way
To navigate this quarrelsome day,
That on the other side of it
I may moor against a quay
Of peace, contentment,
And most of all,
Understanding.

JUNE 17

Fractured light
Of sun
On green tree-tops
Against
A cloud-dark sky
Reminds me:
Even in the
Darkest moments,
There is light;
One simply
Needs
To find it.
Children singing
Raucous songs;
Asphalt backdrop
Of city and street
Reminds me:
Even in the
Quiet of my mind,
There is laugher;
I simply
Need
To find it.

JUNE 18

Rain upon my windowpane;
Summer's opening.
An orchestra of green
Dancing across canopies
Of new-grown leaves,
Thirsty;
Reaching.
I thirst, too:
For the touch of God-hands
Upon my forehead
In welcoming answer
To raised-up prayer;
Offerings poured;
Kneeling knees that prove
Respect, not servitude.
I crave Their love
As Their love craves mine.
Light a candle:
Lightning on the stalli!
Thunder of galdr-song,
Raised to be heard;
Sung to be known.
My heart,
The only drum
That needs beating.

JUNE 19

All work and no play
Makes life the dullest chore.
Children playing
Outside in summer
Awake the child within,
For we all have one.
Most of us just forget
Who they are;
What they look like;
How to play.
Step outside the narrow
Pass that is the grave adult;
Open up the harrow
Cast by all the years built-up.
Release yourself to summer breeze;
To sun on face and skin.
Blow away the dandelions;
Breathe the salt-air in.
All work and no play
Makes life the dullest chore.
As for me, I mean to *live*;
I'll be dead inside no more!

MIDSUMMER

JUNE 20

Wave crash and fire burn;
Build the pyre high!
Midsummer is upon us;
Sunshine fills the sky!
No longer do we sail for distant shores,
Nor pillage treasures as in days of yore,
Yet still we seek out new horizons:
New goals and dreams to explore.
We may not plow the fields with horses,
Nor stow for winter summer morsels,
Yet still we seek to grow:
New ways of thinking and doing restore us.
Wave crash and fire burn;
Build the pyre high!
Midsummer is upon us;
We dance the fire tonight!
Remember all those distant tunes
Of Ancestors singing ancient runes:
Let us join the song!
Remember all those God-stories
Of Aesir and Vanic glories:
Let us join the dance!
Wave crash and fire burn:
Built the pyre high!
Midsummer is upon us;
Sunshine fills the sky!

MIDSUMMER

JUNE 21

I call upon the
Daughters Nine
Of Aegir and of Ran;
Perhaps the Mothers
Of Heimdall,
And perhaps not:
The Nine Waves.
Blodhughadda,
Red-of-hair;
She Who bloodens
Pot-handle,
Blessing it for blot.
Sister, bless.
Bara,
Foam-flecked
Comber;
She who wishes
Yet constrains.
Sister, grant me Will.
Bylgja,
Billow;
She who swells
And roars.
Sister, give me voice.
Dufa,
Pitching Wave;
She who takes
Shape as a dove.
Sister, make me hamr-strong.
Hefring,
Rising Wave;
She who raises up.

Sister, uplift.
Himinglaeva,
Transparent Wave;
She who is
Heaven-Clear.
Sister, gift me with clarity.
Hronn,
Welling Wave;
She who surges and heaps.
Sister, reward.
Kolga,
Cool Wave;
She who cools
And shadows.
Sister, calm.
Unnr,
Frothing Wave;
She who is passionate.
Sister, move me.
Make me heart-strong,
Mind-calm;
Rich in thought and keepings.
Gift me clear-sight,
Happiness;
Journeys and self-esteem.
Make me strong-voiced,
Strong-willed;
Blessed.
Enda er, ok enda skal vera.
Enda er, ok enda skal vera.
Enda er, ok enda skal vera.

MIDSUMMER

JUNE 22

Carry me down,
'Neath waves of wisdom,
Holy Ran;
Not to drown,
But to know.
Show me the
Way of the Lost;
The Foundered;
The Forgotten,
That I may understand.
Help me swim
Against the tides
Of indifference
In this world-above,
Yet not get caught
In the undertow.
Rip-tides of rage
Roil all around us,
Up here under the sun.
Show me how
To deftly swim
Through them and around.
And when calm breaks,
Waves of peace
Crashing against
Nearer shores,
Let me sup
In Aegir's Hall,
With You.

MIDSUMMER

JUNE 23

As evening comes,
I go to wander
Through a castle
Lined with trees.
It's what some might
Call a forest,
But to me, it's just my yard.
It might not seem too special
To the unaware,
But I know its deepest magick;
I know its Landvaettir.
As evening comes,
I go to gather
Leaf and twig and herb;
Every precious flower
Gifted me by earth.
It's what some might
Call a garden,
But to me, it's just my ve.
It might not seem too holy
To the naked eye,
But I know the Gods Who meet here,
And I know that They know me.
As evening comes,
Midsummer's ending,
And I light a sacred flame.
It's what some might
Call a candle,
But to me, it's not so tame.
Instead it is a firebrand
That echoes bright the sun,
To remind me of this Summer's day
Again when Winter comes.

JUNE 24

What lies beneath
What lies below
What lies within:
These I would know.
To look inside
And find peace there:
A gift I'd love to get.
To build frith
With my own
Dear Self;
Pour a cup of kindness
For my heart;
Feed all four parts
Of my breathing soul.
The Ocean understands
That Deep Below;
That numinous depth
That is the beating heart
Of Woman or Man,
Too long adrift.
Hler knows;
He listens.
Aegir feeds the multitude,
Even in the heat
Of winter-borne greed.
I make a gift of bread and beer
For great Aegir.
Feed my soul
With tide's ebb,
And ocean's depth.

What lies beneath
What lies below
What lies within:
These I would know.
To look inside
And find peace there:
A gift I'd love to get.
Gift for gift,
Let there be
Frith between me and Thee.
Blessing for blessing;
Understood to understand.
So let it be.

JUNE 25

Utiseta by the sea:
Breath flows
To tide's ebb;
In and out,
Out and in.
Sand between my toes
And 'neath my seat.
Utiseta by the sea:
Gulls cry out
In hungered passion;
Laugh at jokes
Only Ran knows.
I smile;
Inside out,
Outside in.
Ocean becomes traffic becomes ocean.
By the sea or not,
Utiseta:
I am sea;
Sea is me,
Ebbing and flowing
With each passing breath;
Grit upon my skin
Of ages past
And dust of Kin,
Kith, and Path.
Utiseta by the sea:

JUNE 26

Seawater and glass:
Pour a blot
For the Van.
Father Njordr,
Help me understand
The middle ground;
How to give and take
Yet give again.
Guide me towards
Bright, Right horizons
That will profit me
In more than gold.
May my nets not return
To me empty.
Saltwater on stone:
Set my heart to drink
The bounty of kindness
From my fellow Woman and Man,
That I may return it,
Gift for gift, as with
Seawater and glass.

JUNE 27

Njordr,
Lift me up
From these troubled waters,
And help me find a place
On which to stand.
Teach me the faith
Of the sailor,
Tossed upon the
Stormy sea;
Teach me not to
Fear the horizon,
But to have faith
In what I cannot see.
For wealth comes not
To the faint of heart,
And we are all but
Fishermen,
Casting nets
We hope to find
Filled with bounty
From life's sea.

JUNE 28

Daybreak comes,
And I am opened;
Daybreak comes,
And I am glad.
Somehow,
The world is
Always purer
At the dawning:
Birdsong, and
White-clear sunlight,
Breaking through
Windowpanes
To catch the dust,
And turn it into
Magick.
Daybreak comes,
And I awaken;
Daybreak comes,
And I am glad.
For I take comfort
In the knowing
That there is,
At least,
One more day
To be had.

JUNE 29

Sea-bright;
Beckoning:
She sees
And is seen;
She is,
And ever has been.
Mardoll,
Njordrsdottir:
Amber-teared
Vanadis!
I would cross oceans.
She would cross oceans.
Searching:
I search.
To touch;
Be touched;
To know;
Be known;
To dare;
Be dared;
To will;
Be willed.
Your face
Is tattooed
Upon my heart;
Your magick
Lives
In me.

JUNE 30

Falcon spinning overhead;
Blue woven through the white:
Everything is green.
Paint me feather-skinned;
Flying.
Free me to be me once more.
My Self is a bird,
Caged too long and aching.
Red-gold are my feathers,
Laced with Will and Wisdom.
You, Freyja:
The updraft beneath,
Pushing me ever upwards
And turning the gyre.
Spiralling, I spin;
Spiralling, I find my Self again.
And I am green.
Everything is green.

JULY 1

Cattle in the fields;
Sheep in valleys low,
Grazing.
Green are the reflections
In brown and sleepy eyes;
Green are the reaching arms
Of trees beckoning the sky.
Green the field I walk through;
Green the envious vines,
Which clutch at fence and roadside
And up the stone walls climb.
Green is what I would be:
Green, reclaimed;
Renewed.
Green is what I pray for
As I pour for You:
All-Father breathe me
Green again, and new;
Passion rise and burn again
In ecstasy of You.
Poet, priest of nothing
And everything and Truth:
Green my tongue;
Green my hand;
Green the words that flow.
Green the desperate honesty
Of all the things I wish to know:
Cattle in the fields;
Sheep in valleys low.

JULY 2

Thunder in the mountains
Beneath clouds that hold
Promises of rain:
Everything is made brighter
By a touch of darkness.
Glaesisvellir* mirrors sky;
Echoes back the clouds
And thunder.
Gerdha,
Keeper of the Deathless Acre,**
Plants the seeds of
Sovereignty
Beneath rain-torn clouds
Of Jotunheim,
And in me.
Rain pour;
Cloud burst.
Tears dry;
Heart thirst.
Gerdha:
Plant Your seeds.

*Glaesisvellir: "The Glittering Plain" at the
entrance of Jotunheim.

The Deathless Acre: Udainsakr; encircled by
Glaesisvellir in Jotunheim.

JULY 3

No weapon for Freyr
But love, and the tine
Of a fallow deer.
Yet love was all He needed.
He saw Her there:
Gerdha, Etin-bride;
Garden-dweller fair.
So far away,
And yet as near
As the beating
Of His own heart.
Have you ever felt that?
Have you ever felt
A person so much
A part of you
That just to
Think on them,
Made them real?
Made them close?
So close, you could touch,
If only you could
Be touched in return....
No weapon for me,
But love; perhaps the tine
Of a fallow deer.
For love is all I've needed.

JULY 4

I sing the Sun victorious:
Sunna riding forth,
Wained behind steeds glorious.
I sing the Sun victorious!
Brave and honorable as any
Einherjar, She rides:
Crystal-pure light
Against a sky of blue.
Sunna, ride!
Sunna, renew!
Sunna, celebrate:
The victory of Summer-regained;
The victory of me;
The victory of You!
I sing the Sun victorious:
Sunna riding forth,
Wained behind steeds glorious.
I sing the Sun victorious!
Sunna, ride!
Sunna, shine!
Sunna, renew!

JULY 5

God-gifts
Poured out on me;
God-gifts
I pour.
Gift for gift
Repaid in turn;
Voice raised,
I sing galdr
Clear:
Gebo
I sing
Gebo
Gebo Wunjo
Gebo!
God-gifts
Poured out on me;
God-gifts
I pour.
Gift for gift
Repaid in turn,
And yet
I'm gifted more.
God-gifts
Poured out on me;
God-gifts
Yet I pour.

JULY 6

Blinded by the sun,
Eyes trace patterns
Of bird-flight,
Shadowed,
Against blue sky.
Huginn and Muninn
Fly on black wings:
Ashes upon the
Sunburned clouds.
Black beaks tear
The eyes of memory;
Croak Wyrd into
A language
Never spoken,
Yet understood.
I understand:
I am blind,
Yet I see.
Odin only gave
One eye to the Well.
Yet here I sit,
Blinded by the sun.

JULY 7

I embrace
The enormity
Of the Land;
The Land
Embraces me.
Stone hands
Clutch and reach
Like lovers'
Tongues for
Words that teach.
Numinous
And aching,
The Truth
That is
Our world.
Every Pagan,
A bastard
Who has
Forgotten
Their Mother:
If it be but
Gnosis-unverified
To see
To feel
To know
Such things as this,
Then I would
Dare to know,
Yet remain unproved.

JULY 8

Change rolls in;
It darkens the sky
And moves across the land.
Hagalaz!
Hail to Heimdall and Thor!
Hagalaz
Rides the storm;
It descends with sudden fury.
Hagalaz!
Hail to Heimdall and Thor!
Thunderously,
It tears through the calm;
Breaks the comfortable.
Hagalaz!
Hail to Heimdall and Thor!
In the wake of its arrival,
Hail retreats,
To nourish:
The groundwork
For renewal.
Hagalaz!
Hail to Heimdall and Thor!

--Italicized portions by Jan Tjeerd,
Gifts of the Wyrd

July 9

A thin blue line
Separates Earth
From space;
That vast blackness
Of vacuum and nothing.
A thin blue line
Of smoke rises;
Incense lit on stalli-shelf
To reek a wall
Of separation between
Us and Them:
But who is the Us?
Who is that Them?
Careful,
Lest we raise walls
We were never
Meant to raise.
Careful also,
Lest we raise
No walls at all.
A thin blue line
Separates discernment
From abject prejudice.
Careful,
Lest we move
Across it.

JULY 10

I never found a kind person
Or so goodly a feast,
That it has not been accepted
Hospitably,
Or their money
Nor yet their greed,
A road to reward,
If you please.
Hospitality is the gift,
Not what buys it.
Good company the reward;
You cannot buy true friends.
Greed is a hard road;
All wealth is moveable.
It can just as easily
Wander off tomorrow,
Like cattle without a herder;
Like sheep without a guard.
Love of money
Never gained
A man a friend;
The road to Hel
Is paved with
Good intentions....

--Portions from *Havamal* 39, my own translation.

JULY 11

A friend himself shall prove a friend,
To these and thus a friend;
But [to] his enemy no man owes shelter
Friends to friend be true.
Open the door:
To those who have
Opened the door to you;
To those who have nurtured you
In your time of trouble;
To those of like mind and heart
Who hear you, and understand;
To those who would likewise
Open the door for their fellow humans.
But there is no crime
In sealing shut the door
To those who have likewise slammed
The door on you;
To those who have turned their backs
On you in your time of trouble;
To those who refuse to understand
The heart that beats inside your chest,
Or the mind which thinks inside your head,
And, therefore, refuse to hear you;
To those who would likewise
Slam the door on other fellow humans.
Loyalty is earned.

--Portions from *Havamal* 43, my own translation.

JULY 12

Stand not by while others are wronged.
Let Justice be served.
Look not away as corruption takes hold.
Let Justice be served.
Ignore not the lies; the mockery; the bigotry told.
Let Justice be served.
Courage and boldness from the Sky One to guide
  the way.
Let Justice be served.
Our hands in the mouths of danger,
To protect those in need.
Let Justice be served.
Tyr to guard and guide:
My thoughts;
My words;
My deeds.
I will not stand idle.
I will not be blind.
I will not be ignorant.
I will protect and I will serve
With the courage
Of the Leavings of the Wolf;
With the compassion
Of the Leavings of the Wolf;
With the boldness
Of the Leavings of the Wolf:
Leaving behind only Justice.

--Italicized portions, Jan Tjeerd, *Gifts of the Wyrd*

JULY 13

Dying light erases
Thunder and rain;
Lightning flash
Fades to silhouettes
Of green trees against
Freyr-kissed clouds.
Lord of Light and Shadows;
Of Stair and Mound:
Ignite Your Light in me.
Let me be the one
Who ever strives towards
Peace and good seasons,
In my own life
And in the lives of those
Whom I hold dear.
Let me be
The granter of plenty
In times of need.
Make of my home
A place of frith and hospitality,
For the stranger and the friend.
And at end of day,
As the light is dying,
Let my life be as
Those clouds
After a summer storm:
Freyr-kissed.

JULY 14

The Peace of Njordr to you;
Balance bless your life.
May all of your nets
Be filled with bounty;
All of your horizons bright.
May you navigate fair,
Even through the stormiest seas.
At end of day,
When at last
You find your moorings,
May your sails not need a patch.
And as you lay down
At last to sleep,
May the sea sing you to your rest.
The Peace of Njordr to me;
Balance bless my life.
May all of my nets
Be filled with bounty;
All of my horizons bright.
May I navigate fair,
Even through the stormiest seas.
At end of day,
When at last
I find my moorings,
Let my sails not need a patch.
And as I lay me down
At last to sleep,
May the sea sing me to my rest.

JULY 15

O Sunwise and brilliant day!
The same sun shines down
On the wicked as the strong;
Upon the good as on the wrong.
Illuminate my path!
Show me the snares
Laid out for me,
That I should not be caught.
As the deer
Scents the hunter
On a breeze,
Let me be
Cunning likewise.
Sun shine to reveal
My enemies' designs.
And should the worst
Befall me,
And wickedness be done,
Let Justice shine forth
Brighter even than the Sun!

JULY 16

Fading light
Casts shadows,
On the heath
And in the glen;
Quietly I ponder
How they creep
The same
In hearts of Men.
How does such
Darkness take hold?
What poverty
Of happiness
Must there be,
For someone to
Forsake charity
In favor of greed?
To forego love
For sake of hate?
To withhold hospitality,
Shunning those in need?
Even at night,
The sun is somewhere.
Why not likewise
In people's hearts?
I cannot understand;
Yet this the one
Full wisdom I crave not.

JULY 17

Changing face
Of growing moon:
I am enlarged
By the fulfilling
Of promises;
The keeping
Of oaths.
Let my face
Likewise
Be enlarged,
Yet unchanging.
Tyr,
Bless me
With Honor.
Changing face
Of waning moon:
Make small
The shadows
Of injustice;
The breaking
Of oaths.
Let my face
Remain unshadowed.
Forseti,
Guide me
Toward Justice.

JULY 18

Dagaz
Sowilo Wunjo Inguz
Algiz Jera
Othala
I direct the power of change
Through my own will,
That there be wholeness
Forged in cleansing fire.
Harmony reigns,
And freedom,
Beneath the shield
Of my Gods.
Peace and good seasons come;
A bright inheritance,
Forged by the honor
Of my Ancestors,
Both Kith and Kin.
Dagaz
Sowilo Wunjo Inguz
Algiz Jera
Othala.

JULY 19

I lay my prayers
At Ullr's feet
In summer:
Glory to You
Who is Glory.
Sif-son,
Bathe me
In the radiance
Of victory;
Crown me
With bones,
Rune-etched;
Galdr-strong.
Teach me to
Hunt for Truth,
Dignity, and
Honor.
Strengthen
My arms;
My sight;
My heart.
Set me to
Glide
Through life
With the
Ease of skis.
Unblock
My pathways.
Hail, Ullr!

JULY 20

With virtue I walk.
A virtuous road lays before me:
With honor may I walk.
A virtuous road lays behind me:
Fully knowing my Self may I walk.
A virtuous road lays below me:
I offer hospitality as I walk.
A virtuous road lays above me:
With wisdom may I walk.
A virtuous road lays beside me:
In loyalty may I walk.
A virtuous road lays all around me:
In trust may I walk.
Virtuous roads reach in all directions:
In humility may I walk.
Many virtuous roads, to many virtuous worlds:
With courage may I walk.
Other virtuous people walk these roads with me:
Bringing justice may I walk.
With virtue I walk.
Walk on!

JULY 21

I sing a song
Of my Self
To my Self,
Sacrificed
As Odin
On the Tree:
I have been
Pierced
By the spears
Of indignation;
By the harsh words
Of those
Who would judge,
Neither fairly
Nor rightly.
No bread
They gave to me;
No horns offered,
In my time
Of need.
I sing a song
Of my Self
To my Self,
Sacrificed
As Odin
On the Tree:
Let me gain
Wisdom from this,
Yet never pain.

JULY 22

I need not be
What others want,
Yet let me be
What is needed
When need haunts
The hearts and mouths
Of those craving
To be fed;
Let me be the teacher,
Worthy to the task,
When student seeks,
Craving to be led.
I need not meet
The definitions
Inflicted by those
Who would try
To take my power,
But do not truly know
Me for me,
Nor I for I.
Yet let me surpass
The expectations
Of my Gods in all I do,
For all that
Ultimately matters
Is what
Matters Ultimately.

JULY 23

I sing a new song
For the days
Still yet to come,
And yet for days gone-by;
For the old and the new;
The tried and the Tru;
For all those new beginnings
That were endings
At their start.
I galdr into art
The pain and the pleasure;
The wisdom without measure
That lives in questions
Yet unasked;
Answers, yet ungiven.
I sing a new song
For the children yet unborn,
And the adults who will raise them
And raise them up.
Please, raise them up!
I sing a new song
For my Gods Who are my shield;
For the soldier in the field;
For the teacher in the classroom,
And the nurse who heals.
I sing a new song.

JULY 24

Days go by so slowly,
Yet still I am
Here and breathing;
Such a blessing!
How often we forget
To thank the Gods
For the simplest
Of things,
So caught up are we
In the asking;
In petitions for our needs,
When really,
All we need
Is to breathe.
To breathe,
And yet be breath
For those who find themselves
Crushed in the
Narrows of life.
Days go by so slowly,
Yet still I am
Here and breathing;
Such a blessing!
Thank you, Gods!

JULY 25

Grant me the strength,
I pray,
To go the distance
In defense of what I love;
To act with honor,
Even in the face
Of great adversity.
Give me the drive
To do my best,
Not for any pride of my own
In the doing of such things,
But that I may make
My family proud;
My beloveds proud;
My friends proud;
My Gods proud.
Let my glory be shared
With those who
Fight alongside me
In the good fight
For what is Right and Just.
And when the way is dark,
Let me raise my head and sing
Eihwaz Eihwaz Eihwaz .
In Ydalir,*
May I be refreshed with glory.

*Ydalir: The Yew Dales, home of Ullr.

JULY 26

Let ours not be
An inheritance
Of shame:
Tear down the
Banners of bigotry,
Othala to reclaim!
End the slavery
Of obsession
With the differences of Men:
I care not your gender,
Nor the color of your skin.
Neither did my Ancestors.
I only care about what happens
Inside your heart.
If it beats with compassion,
And harbors not hate,
I stand with you.
Let ours not be
An inheritance
Of shame:
Tear down the
Banners of bigotry;
Othala reclaim!

JULY 27

Pull a stave
For Justice
That needs doing;
Another,
For the resolution.
Mystery unweave:
Waves of Wyrd
Be parted,
That I may see
Where in this world
I am needed;
Who in this world
Needs me.
Let me rise
To the task at hand;
Provide me, I pray,
A well-laid plan
For doing those things
Which act as tests
Of those oaths
I've sworn to protect.
Pull a stave
For Justice;
Another,
For the resolution.
Mystery unweave.

JULY 28

Strength:
In my times of weakness,
And in those times
When I need to be strong
Because others cannot.
Make me the shoulder
That can be cried on;
The arms that hold,
When anguish crashes over
And bodies are wracked
With tears.
Let me be the Great Consoler;
A comfort,
As is Sigyn;
As is Freyja;
As is Frigga;
As is Odin;
As is Thor;
As is Tyr.
Strength:
As mountains are strong;
As rock, as it aches against water.
Help me,
That I may not only endure,
But assist others to do likewise.

JULY 29

The oak in June
Was barely dressed;
Now, it reaches
Green fingers towards
Summer lightning
As though aching
To be touched.
I reach for You,
Lord Freyr!
Green-fingered;
Aching,
Like a summer tree,
I reach for You.
Grant me the peace
Of this good season;
Make fertile my life
With those gifts
That I have
Worked hard to earn.
Dress me as
That summer tree:
Cloaked in green hope;
Bright with promise
Of suns not yet risen,
And days still to come.
Hail Freyr!

JULY 30

Teach me how to speak
Words that heal instead of harm;
Thor Plain-Speaker,
Make of me a Farmer of Wo/Men:
One who plants seeds
And yet cares for them,
Nurturing the sprouts that grow
In minds and in hearts,
Because of the words
That I have planted.
Bring down the rains
Of strength and hope,
That they may water
Those deeds which
Follow my words:
Keep me true to
Those things spoken.
Let me be known as
Keeper-of-Words:
A person who
Walks their talk.

JULY 31

Hope harbors not
Doubts to plague
The mind by night,
Nor worry to meet the day.
Hope harbors not
Dark-tinged clouds
Around the heart
That hold us back
From promise.
Hope harbors not
These things, and yet
Sometimes we cling to them
Too closely;
Too blindly.
Rather than set
Our thoughts upon
The greenness of the grass
After the storm,
We focus only on the hail.
Rather than set
Our hearts upon
Gilded tables for the Aes,
We hear only
Heimdall's horn.

AUGUST 1

Horsefields,
Plentiful of grain and grass,
Stretch
Into the West.
Wind on my face
Smells of oats
And promises.
Brother and Sister,
Bring me home!
Freyr and Freyja,
Know my name!
Let it be sung
In Sessrumnir
With notes of Honor.
And when that
Time comes,
That I should
Be removed
From this world--
This mortal vale,
Of tears and woes--
Bring me to
Folkvangr,
Head held high;
Chosen of the
Vanir.

AUGUST 2

By your Hallowed Names,
I charge this rune:
Fehu.
Freyr's Rune;
Cattle-rune;
Rune of movable wealth.
Sign of hope and plenty,
Success and happiness.
I carve you thus;
With your help, I advise against loss, cowardice,
    and stupidity.
I paint you the green of growing things;
I prove you through abundance, gain, and right
    ownership.
I pray you: *Please*.
I blot you with green and growing things.
I send you forth as peace and good seasons for
    myself;
Peace and good seasons for those I hold dear.

AUGUST 3

I come,
At the cusp of August,
To celebrate
The wane and The Wain.
Summer bleeds slowly
Into Autumn;
One last harvest
Of leaf and green.
Vanir ride towards Alfheim!
Lord of Light
Becomes
Lord of Shadow;
Of Mound and Ancestor.
Vanir ride towards Alfheim!
Tides ebb stormy,
With promise of hurricane
And icy winter seas.
Njordr be our navigator,
And our guide.
Vanir ride towards Alfheim!
And as we come
To foot of Spiral Stair,
Let us take a moment
To tarry there,
Remembering
All those things
We planted in the Spring
Which grew through Summer.
Ride, Vanir, ride!

AUGUST 4

I prepare for winter:
One last sweet delight
In Summer's bliss;
One last lingering embrace
Of Summer's kiss.
Days grow long,
And hot, and humid.
Buzz of cicada;
Call of crow
Remind us:
What has gone before
Will come again.
The work we've done outside
Soon moves within:
The planting of seeds
In good earth
Replaced with
The planting of souls
For rebirth
That comes
In so many
Myriad ways:
Renewal of vows and oaths;
Knowledge of the Self.
Knowing where we've been
Shows us the way forward.
I am ready to begin.

AUGUST 5

Arms open wide
And spinning:
Final spiral dance
Of bees,
Drawing down the Sun.
Shine on!
Shine on!
Though May be far behind,
And Winter at our door.
Shine on!
Shine on!
My heart burns
As the asphalt
In August haze;
Scent of tar and ozone.
My heart burns
For the Gods
Of Summer Days
And Winter's Promise.
Shine on!
Shine on!
Though May be far behind,
And Winter at our door.
Shine on!
Shine on!
I raise my inner light
To the world,
And I dance.

FREYRFAXI

AUGUST 6

That horse was slate grulla of color,
Who Hrafnkell called Freyrfaxi.
Hrafnkell gave Freyr, his friend,
Half the horse in that way.
For this horse Hrafnkell had
So much love, that he swore
That he should have to kill
Any man who rode Freyrfaxi
Against his will.
Let it be the will of Freyr
That I grab tight the mane
Of the horse that is Heilag-Vilja;
That I may ride across the Worlds,
Faring-forth on behalf
Of Justice and a fair Wyrd
For myself, and for those
Whom I hold dear.
Let me come to love
Both horse and rider,
For it is always worse
For the one being ridden.
Set the grar-hest* beneath me:
That I may ride the course with Freyr
From Summer's Light,
Into the Mound of Winter.

--Portions from *Hrafnkels Saga Freyrsgodha*,
translation mine.

*grar-hest: "grey horse"; Grey horses, and
especially dappled-grey horses, are frequently
featured as psychopomps in Norse Lore.

FREYRFAXI

AUGUST 7

Hail Holy Freyr!
The light is dimming
At end of day;
Scattered birds
Beweep the sun,
Setting on the horizon.
Soon is winter come;
Soon the Mound Your dwelling.
You climb the Spiral Stair
To Alfheim's height,
To once more leave behind
Vanaheim's fields of plenty.
We thank You for
The harvest now at hand;
The gleaning of the fruits
From field and Wo/Man.
In gratitude with
Bended knees we pour
One last offering,
Yet again one first.
Hail Holy Freyr!
At the dimming of the day,
Yet shines Your Light.
Hail Ingvi-Freyr!
Peace and good seasons to You,
And to us, and to all those
Whom we hold dear.

FREYRFAXI

AUGUST 8

The last turn of the leaf;
Fruits of vine and
Plant and field
Feel no grief
As they are
Gathered home.
May it be
Likewise for us:
Joy for the Ancestors
Awaiting us soon,
As we approach
The cusp of September.
Dance!
Dance for those carried home!
To Helheim and Folkvangr;
Aegir's Hall and Sessrumnir.
Even to the lofty halls
Of Valhalla and Himinbjorg;
Songs for those who have
Climbed the Spiral Stair!
Leaves change,
As do we.
Seasons fade,
One into another,
As we become
More our Selves,
Each to each other.

AUGUST 9

Ears pricked low;
Listening:
Was there ever
So loyal a creature
As the horse?
Velvet-muzzled
Nuzzles soothe;
Remind us
How breath
Unites us all.
Your air is mine;
Mine is yours.
Each exhalation
An inhalation
Of connectedness.
We are all
Companions
On a shared road;
Though our journeys
Be quite different.
Let my ears
Be pricked low;
Listening.
Was there ever
So loyal a creature
As am I?

AUGUST 10

By your Hallowed Names,
I charge this rune:
Hagalaz.
Heimdall's Rune;
Hail-Rune;
Rune of nature's wrath.
Sign of destruction and controlled crisis;
Of testing and trial which lead to inner harmony.
I carve you thus;
With your help, I advise against catastrophe,
    stagnation, suffering, and pain.
I paint you the white of summer ice;
I prove you by accepting those things which are
    beyond my control.
I pray you: *Help*.
I blot you with ice and rainwater.
I send you forth as harmony in the face of
    opposition for myself;
Harmony in the face of opposition for those I hold
    dear.

Connla Freyjason

AUGUST 11

Stormfront blows against
A horizon torn open
By lightning flash.
Thor comes riding:
Wain-bound, like a Van;
Mjollnir raised to
Hallow and to smite.
Pass softly;
Speak kindly,
Though thunder roar
And lightning flash.
Bring the rain,
To kiss the sweet grass
With Your blessings,
Hallowing all
Within Your path.
And when the calm comes,
Let it leave me
Knowing Your presence:
Eternal and renewing as
Tanngnjostr and Tanngrisnir.*

*Tanngnjostr and Tanngrisnir: the goats which
pull Thor's chariot. He routinely eats them, and
then resurrects them with Mjollnir.

AUGUST 12

Line, cast;
Hook, baited:
I plant myself,
Firmly and prepared,
As Thor in ship's prow,
Beside Hymir.
And I am wait-ful
And eager-hearted.
I crave to catch
And to capture
That space outside all spaces;
That time outside all times.
Jormungandr,
Let us dance
Those old familiar
Yet forgotten steps
Of fisherman and prey:
Of Thor and the Serpent,
As it thrashed,
Threatening
To carry Him away.
Thus carry me:
Away, yet deeper,
Within my Self;
With my Gods,
And You.

AUGUST 13

I need and I am needed;
I am wanted, yet I want.
In this space I come,
To know and yet be known.
Let there be peace and knowing;
Let there be Truth well-kenned.
Deep within the quiet spaces,
You are there;
My I is made We.
I am made small
By the respect I owe You.
I am enlarged
By the love bestowed.
I come in prayer,
Yet find conversation:
We speak without words
What only the heart knows.
You need and You are needed;
You are wanted, yet You want.
And We are here;
Together.

AUGUST 14

Red-Gold
The leaves are turning;
Softly, just now,
But wait....
Acorns pepper roof
And ground,
A steady rat-tat-tat
For Ratatosk's children.
Plenty present,
All around.
The Earth's last harvest
Has not yet given
Up its ghost.
Red-Gold
You come to me
On autumn breezes
First whispered
Through baring trees,
Laying my heart bare
To Your passion
For Your Lover,
Once again
Wandered away.

AUGUST 15

Summer's dance is nearly over;
Autumn's dance, just begun.
Birds and breeze sing now
A different tune.
Gone the calls from mate to mate,
Flirting in the sun;
Now the calls of journeys made,
Heading toward the South.
Geeze fly in wide v's
Against skies so blue they blind me:
Kenaz and Kenaz and Kenaz.
The world manifests once more:
This time in shades
Of dark and violent hue;
Of violet nights bleeding
Into crimson days.
I burn with the humidity
Of aching, hanging Summer,
Its death-grip fingers
Scraping for one last hurrah.
Summer's dance is nearly over;
Autmn's dance, just begun.
And I, the dancer;
Poised, and ready
To begin.
Again.

AUGUST 16

Once I was a child
Upon a summer hill,
Fresh-faced and reaching.
I reach still:
To Gods,
Above and Below;
Kingly Gods,
Full of Wisdom and Poetry;
Strong Gods,
Backs bowed from hands
Colored by tilling good earth;
Compassionate Gods,
Who know my agony
And understand;
Devouring Gods,
Elemental and sometimes
Unforgiving,
But only sometimes.
Once I was a child
Upon a summer hill,
Fresh-faced and reaching.
I reach still.

AUGUST 17

Nornir
Bend Your ears to me;
Nornir
Lend Your eyes.
Nornir
Teach Your gifts to me;
Nornir
Do not despise:
This restless child
Of Wyrd's whimsy,
Lost upon the flow
Of Hamingja and Orlog.
Nornir
Bend Your ears to me;
Nornir
Lend Your eyes.
Nornir
Teach Your gifts to me;
Nornir
Do not despise:
Blessings I bring,
And humble pourings;
Offerings for gifts bestowed,
And gifts unexpected.
Nornir
Bend Your ears to me;
Nornir
Lend Your eyes....

AUGUST 18

Thorns grow sharpest
In that depth of Summer
Where Will and Wisdom
Collide against a backdrop
Of bleeding sky
And coming promise.
Rains bleed down windowpanes
Caked in dust from inside;
Smokey eyes upon
A world that is slowly burning.
These, the last tears of Thor
For the growing-season,
Echoing the tears of those of us
With so much inside
That still needs growing.
We must be cautious of the thorns.
They prick to bleed us dry
Of hope and emotion;
Of basic charity that prevents us
From crushing another Wo/Man's dignity.
Ever so careful of the thorns.
They grow sharpest
In this depth of Summer;
Will and Wisdom colliding
Against a backdrop of bleeding sky.

AUGUST 19

By your Hallowed Names,
I charge this rune:
Tiwaz.
Tyr's Rune;
Sky-Rune;
Rune of honor, justice, and the law.
Sign of leadership and authority;
Of rationality, self-sacrifice, and victory in legal
    matters.
I carve you thus;
With your help, I advise against dishonor,
    disloyalty, and authoritative domination.
I paint you the red and green of spear and oak;
I prove you each time I recognize my own strength
    and act with integrity.
I pray you: *Honor*.
I blot you with oath-keeping, bread, and fine stew.
I send you forth as honor, justice, and victory for
    myself;
Honor, justice, and victory for those I hold dear.

AUGUST 20

Sweet sacrifice:
To give up all those
Ties that bind us
To the tyranny
Of the past.
Sloughing off
Aged ideals,
Fostered by years
Of ingraining.
My experience is mine.
Let my expression be likewise:
Uniquely personal;
All my own.
A voice,
Laced with
Honor and dignity,
Raised to Gods
Who live,
Not merely
In the pages
Of some dusty tome,
But in the world
And through me.

AUGUST 21

I will not be ashamed
Of my service to the Gods
Simply because you say so.
Who are you,
To tell me such a thing;
To make divine pronouncement?
Who pours your blot?
Who wrote your name
In Eddas at a time
When to do so
Might mean death?
I will not be ashamed
Of my service to the Gods
Simply because you think that's
"Too Christian".
Tell that to our Ancestors,
Lying in graves on distant heaths,
Surrounded by the symbols
Of their service;
Buried in a time
Long before the Church
Reached their lands.
I will not be ashamed
Of my service to the Gods:
I am not a slave to Them;
I simply serve, as I do
For all my friends.

August 22

We cannot say
Our community
Should not judge us:
How else could we
Save face?
How else could we
Understand
Honor, dignity;
The need to defend
Our fellow Wo/Man?
But to judge righteously,
One must be
Equipped righteously:
One must know compassion.
One must know charity.
One must crave peace, not war.
One must not eschew love.
One must understand Hamingja.
Without these,
It is not a true community:
It is a mob.
I *can* say
A mob
Should not judge us:
I *do* say it.
With pride,
I shout it
To my Gods.

AUGUST 23

Stop holding back!
Stop measuring your
Words, thoughts, actions,
Against the sensibilities
Of others.
You know what you know;
Believe what you believe;
Love who you love,
And Who you love.
Love pure.
Believe pure.
Know pure:
Know without bounds,
Ever-thirsting for more
And more knowledge.
Quench your thirst
With so much more
Than books!
Some things must be
Experienced
To be known:
The taste of a berry
Sweet on the vine;
The touch of a God's hand
With your own, intertwined.
Know pure.
Believe pure.
Love pure.

AUGUST 24

Love is not pure
When coupled
With judgment;
When practiced
Despite,
Not because.
Pure love
Sparks joy
In the knowing
That you know
And yet
Are known;
That you embrace,
And yet
Are embraced.
Such bliss is a
Blot-of-itself,
Love to Love,
And to the Gods.
Pure love
Looks past
The surfaces
Of things,
Toward what lies
Within.
It is a
Deeper thing.
Dig.

AUGUST 25

I do not give
Because I have to;
I do not give
In requirement.
I do not give
In exchange
For that which I might get.
Reciprocity
Works differently
Than some people
Might think.
I do not give
To make myself important;
I do not give
To impress Wo/Man or Gods.
I do not give
To scare the neighbors;
I do not give
Because I want to be
A Viking "when I grow up".
I have no time
For such childishness.
Gift-for-gift,
I give for
Love.

AUGUST 26

Raise your sword
And scream
If you have to;
Shoulder against
The shield-wall,
Knees bent
In constant aching
Against the strain
Of trying to maintain
The status quo
Of "you against the world".
Raise your sword
And scream,
If you have to.
I will pity
Your exhaustion,
But I will not
Raise my own,
Unless there be
Injustice
Which calls me,
Sword to bear.
Then I will
Raise my sword
And scream
If I have to;
Shoulder against
The shield-wall,
Knees bent

In constant aching
Against the strain
Of defending
Humankind.
Those who crave
Only glory
Rarely find it;
When we paint
The world with
Monsters,
Monsters are
The only ones
Who truly get
To live.
Raise your sword
And scream,
If you have to.
But I will not
Raise my own
Unless I must;
Unless I find myself
Called to battle
By the Gods,
In Whom I put
My trust.

AUGUST 27

I manifest
My own Power:
Apathy
Has no place here;
Preconceptions
Hold no sway.
Today is a
Brand new day!
Once upon a time,
I cared
What others thought;
I worried
They would judge me,
Shun me,
Hurt me.
Ultimately,
They stole me from me.
No more!
I manifest
My own Power:
I am bright;
I am shining;
My mind and heart
Are clear!
I am Heidhr;
I shine!
Shine on!

AUGUST 28

Sun dips
Rain drips
Wolves howl
Time slips:
I stand
At the edge.
It is not
Ragged,
As some
Have said,
But bright-clear
Instead.
Cat mews
Many-colored hues
Against backdrop
Of blackened
Sky:
I stand
At the edge.
And I fly.

AUGUST 29

Ing
Ablaze with promise;
Burning in the
Heart of August.
Winternights,
Too soon upon us,
Beckon us
Within.
Freyr
Climbs the Stair
That is both
Up and Down.
Ing
Ablaze.
All hail to the
Lord of Grain and Grave!
Ing
Ablaze.
Burn sweet,
With autumn fire!
Freyr
Climbs the Stair
That is both
Up and Down.
All hail to the
Lord of Grain and Grave!

AUGUST 30

Preach bliss to me:
Not some long-forgotten
Story, past its time;
Nor some saga of blood and glory,
Which has escaped its prime.
Teach bliss to me:
Bliss and blessings
Wrought by hands
That I cannot see
With my two eyes,
Yet know well inside my heart.
Unleash bliss for me:
Pour it as freely
As blot upon the ve;
As rain upon the empty fields
Of harvest.
Reach bliss with me:
Come together,
Heart to hand
And forward-looking;
Man to Woman and
Woman to Man.
Preach bliss to me:
Words of love
Experienced
In divine groves
Woven by intent,
Rather than by trees.

AUGUST 31

Peace and bright blessings given;
Peace and bright blessings gained.
Such is frith.
Peace is a thing
We must build;
Walls only exist
To hold it inside.
Peace and bright blessings given;
Peace and bright blessings gained.
Let us not resolve
To shut out the hidden;
The weak or the shamed.
Instead, a hand,
In friendship,
That trust and frith be gained.
Peace and bright blessings given;
Peace and bright blessings gained.
Gift-for-gift
We only garnish
What we've earned.
Let that bright
Payment be received as
Peace and bright blessings given;
Peace and bright blessings gained.

Fire to Ice,
The Wheel
Turns....

THE SEASON OF ICE

WINTERNIGHTS, ALFABLOT, YULE, DISABLOT, SIGRBLOT

SEPTEMBER 1

Up the Stair
And Underground;
Lord of Alfheim;
Lord of Mound!
Hail Freyr!
As the Wheel turns,
May we look
Within,
And not find
Darkness there.
Whatever work
That must be done,
May Light guide us
To make things
Right once more.
Up the Stair
And Underground;
Lord of Alfheim;
Lord of Mound!
Hail Freyr!

SEPTEMBER 2

Protect us
From the gale;
From storm-surge
And hurricane-flare;
From hail-storm
And lightning's glare.
Thor bless and
Thor hallow:
With rain that falls,
To quench the thirst
Of man and beast
And urgent earth;
With lightning-strike
To light the night,
Yet cause no harm
When falling.
Thor hallow and
Thor bless:
Teach us words
Of frithful peace;
Make our words
Match our deeds.
I cast Mjollnir
Against a blackened sky:
Hail Thor!
Protect us!

SEPTEMBER 3

I sing a song
Of sow and boar:
Hildisvini,
Cloak of Ottar;
Syr, to Whom
He kept Hogr.
Hail Freyja!
Let the stones
Of my ve
Run red for You:
Blot-dyed,
From wine and juice;
From sweet things
Left for You.
Hail Freyja!
Don the feathers
Of Fjadhrhamr;
Wisely choose
Among the slain.
Valfreyja!
While I seek,
I do not summon;
Rather, pay respect.
And beg to be
Cloaked as Ottar,
When I need You
To protect.
I sing a song
Of sow and boar:
Hildisvini; Sacred Syr!

September 4

I claim my inheritance:
Ancestors,
Both kith and kin,
Down the long line
Of what has been;
I claim my inheritance.
More pride in
Who I could be
Than in who I am,
I claim my inheritance.
No matter the
Color of my skin:
I claim my inheritance.
As the worthy sibling
Of all Wo/Men:
I claim my inheritance.
Regardless of whom
I give my heart:
I claim my inheritance.
Loving others
As I love my Gods:
I claim my inheritance.
Quick to speak up
For the needful weak:
I claim my inheritance.
Bringing Justice
For those who
Have been wronged
By those who sneer
In demeaning tones:
I claim my inheritance.

SEPTEMBER 5

Cleanse
My heart,
My mind,
My tongue:
Of wrong-minded
Attitudes;
Of judgmental
Platitudes;
Of blanket statements
That assume,
And expressions
Of ingratitude.
Thor, help me speak plain;
Sif, help me speak kind.
Njordr, help me keep peace;
Freyr, help me to shine.
Freyja, teach me
The endurance
Of Gullveig,
When there is
Need of it;
That I may burn thrice,
Yet be reborn.
Make me
Heidhr:
Bright,
Shining,
Clear.
Enda er, ok enda skal vera.

SEPTEMBER 6

Ever-blessed
Be my altar;
Ever-blessed
Be my life.
Ever-blessed
Each good husband;
Ever-blessed
Each good wife.
Ever-blessed
In the morning;
Ever-blessed
By noon-day,
And when dusk
Comes a-falling,
Ever-blessed
Let me stay.
Ever-blessed
The trees, as they shed
Leaves in splendor;
Ever-blessed
The earth,
As we meander
Towards winter.
Ever-blessed
Be my altar;
Ever-blessed
Be my ve.
Ever-blessed
May life find me;
Ever-blessed
May I stay.

SEPTEMBER 7

Fire manifests
In turning leaves,
As trees die-to-live
Again in Spring.
Autumn touches
Everything;
My heart, no less.
Sif's hair
Has been let down,
Veiling sunsets
In gold.
Frithful strands
Blow across faces,
Otherwise unknown.
Fire manifests
In embers laid
In cauldron and
On hearth.
Warmth touches
Everything;
My heart, no less.
Frigga's keys
Have been hung
By the lintel
Of my heart's
Doorway.
I am home;
I welcome my Gods.

SEPTEMBER 8

The first-laid feast
Of fall fruits
Beckons from the table:
Pumpkin and apple;
Pecan and corn.
I raise a glass
To my Ancestors:
May you rest well,
In Whoever's Hall
You live,
For to me,
You ever-will.
To me, and
Through me, and
With me,
Through all my days,
And days-to-come.
For those whose
Blood I share:
Skal! Gods-be-with-you!
For those who
Nurtured me in
Troubled times:
Skal! Gods-be-with-you!
For those who
Set me on my Path,
Who still guard and guide:
Skal! Gods-be-with-you!
For those who
Gave their lives
That I might live free:

Skal! Gods-be-with-you!
For those who
Suffered persecution
That I might
Live my Truth:
Skal! Gods-be-with-you!
For those who
Loved this land,
Long before I ever
Walked upon it:
Skal! Gods-be-with-you!
For those who
Have no one else left
To raise a glass
In remembrance:
Skal! Gods-be-with-you!
As I enjoy
This first-laid feast
Of fall fruits,
I pray that you will never hunger;
I pray that you will never thirst.
And for my descendants,
And your own,
Whoever and wherever
They may be:
May they never hunger;
May they never thirst.
Blessings to the Blessed
For their blessings bestowed;
Blessings to the blessed
For our blessings still owed.
Enda er, ok enda skal vera.
Enda er, ok enda skal vera.
Enda er, ok enda skal vera.
Blessed be.

SEPTEMBER 9

Harvest moon
Shine down on me;
Golden light
Hallow even the inmost
Edges of my heart.
Let me be frithful;
Easy-living;
Kind.
Freyr,
Gift me with peace,
And good seasons.
Gerdha,
Bless the harvests
Of my heart,
That they not
Be lacking.
Nerthus,
Kiss me,
As You kiss the Earth,
That I may grow again,
Come Spring.
Plant me
As a bulb
In the dirt:
The promise
Of a flower,
Cloaked in
Darkling garb.

September 10

Birch waxes gold
In autumn,
Mirror of the hair
Of Sif;
Hue of the keys
Of Frigga;
Bright as the mane
Of Gullinbursti
As Freyr rides
Toward Alfheim-gate.
May there be
Frithful peace
As the leaves fall;
May there be
Frithful peace
In each home and hall.
May there be
Frithful peace
Beneath mound and harrow;
May there be
Frithful peace
On each dawning morrow.
May there be
Frithful peace.

SEPTEMBER 11

Remembrance
Is a dark bird
With flashing wings
That perches
In the heart
To croak songs
Sometimes
Sorrowful.
Yet often
Filled with
Wisdoms
Yet unsung.
Oh, my Lords;
My Ladies:
Let me remember!
Let me be
Remembered,
Better still,
That the Raven
Not croak
Tear-songs
For my
Descendants.
Instead,
Bright caws
Of hope and
Will and
Wisdom.

SEPTEMBER 12

Sun-drenched,
My ve, even beneath
The scattered leaves
Of trees aching
Towards winter.
I sweep the cobwebs
With my hands
And pour for You:
Oh, Gods, my Gods!
My gratitude is
Boundless as the sun.
I thirst for You,
Yet find myself quenched;
I hunger for You,
Yet find myself fed.
Others say they
Do not kneel,
And will not,
Yet I find myself
Often on my knees:
Sometimes, as now,
To clean my ve;
Others, out of love
And respect.
Oh, Gods, my Gods!
I thirst for You;
Yet find myself quenched;
I hunger for You,
Yet find myself fed.
And I kneel.

SEPTEMBER 13

Thunder of rain
Upon the roof
Loud as the
Thunder of hooves:
Thor comes,
In gilded chariot
Pulled by goats,
As much wain-rider
As any Van!
Einridhi*,
Give me strength
To endure loneliness;
Hardhhugadhr*,
Make my heart
Brave like Yours.
Sonnungr*,
Keep me Tru
As are You;
Vethormr*,
Protect my sacred space;
My hearth, stalli, and ve.
Veurr*,
Hallow my life
And the lives
Of all those whom
I hold dear.

*By-names of Thor (in order): "Lone-rider";
"Tough-Courage" or "Hard-Hearted"; "True One"
or "True Youth"; "Shrine-Thor"; "Holy-Warder" or
"Hallower".

September 14

Curve of antler,
Bone and horn;
Bite of spear,
Wind, and thorn:
Autumn comes swiftly.
Even stones weep
For Spring,
As metal weeps
Against frost.
May the chill
Remain outside;
Let not my
Heart be hardened.
May I weep
As freely as
Frigga for Baldur,
When time comes
For emotions
To be shown.
Let me freely
Feel my feelings,
Knowing that my
Gods are my shield:
Vulnerability,
A strength
That shield affords.

SEPTEMBER 15

Blessings
And God-connections
May I find;
Runes
And advising symbols
To bind and
Unbind.
Ansuz
Draw upon
My windowsill:
Blessings and Gods
Be gained!
Ansuz
Let me sing
Beneath the
Lintel of my doorway:
Blessings and Gods
Be gained!
Ansuz
Before the hearth
That is this home's heart:
Blessings and Gods
Be gained!
Blessings
And God-connections
May I find;
Runes
And advising symbols
To bind and
Unbind.

SEPTEMBER 16

Hope
To heal my burdens;
Hope
To cleanse my mind:
Of troubles and of worries
And of thoughts unkind.
Hope
To create new ways
To bless and celebrate
My Gods and Their Creation:
This world in which I co-create.
Hope
To soothe my heart,
When it is pulled apart;
Hope
To see a new dawn
Even in the deepest Dark.
Hope
To encircle;
Hope
To surround:
My life,
My home,
My family;
All those who
I cannot imagine
My life without.

SEPTEMBER 17

My heart endures,
As Sigyn:
Needful of compassion
Against a storm
Of tyranny.
Let such not
Overhang us,
As a veil of clouds,
Dark and dangerous.
Instead,
Thor's shroud:
Clouds full of
Promise and rebirth;
Storms of
Regeneration.
My heart endures,
As Hardhhugadhr*:
Hard,
Not for lack of feeling,
But for abundance
Of strength.
I will not shatter;
I will not break,
Though I be
Needful of compassion;
Though my heart
Might ache.

*A by-name of Thor: "Tough-Courage" or "Hard-Hearted"

SEPTEMBER 18

Shoulders curve
Against the rising chill,
As an aurochs
Braced against cold weather.
Frost creeps
Across my windowsill,
Painting the world
White and wonderful
Before Skadi and Holda
Ever even think
Of snow.
Isa Uruz:
Hold fast,
Hold strong.
Isa Uruz:
For Winter comes,
And Summer's gone.
Isa Uruz.
I cuddle blankets
In the heart
Of September,
And I await
The long nights
To come.

WINTERNIGHTS

SEPTEMBER 19

Þá skyldi blóta í móti vetri til árs:
There should be a blot towards
The setting in of winter
For a good year.
That time has come.
Let it be a gift to us,
Filled with harvests
Of gratitude.
Let us sing:
Gebo.
May we be gifted with goodly things
Equally in the year to come
As we have been gifted with goodly things
In the year soon-gone.
We raise a glass for Odin:
All-Father,
Whom we love;
Whom we respect.
Skal!
We raise a glass for
Freyr and Njordr:
Peace and good seasons to us,
And to those who come after,
And to all those whom we hold dear.
Skal!

*Portions from *Ynglinga Saga*, my own translation.

WINTERNIGHTS

SEPTEMBER 20

This is the first and last;
The last and first.
We stand at the doorway
Of another Wheel-turn;
Everything ends
And begins
Again.
This is the first and last;
The last and first.
Our cups are filled
To quench Gods-thirst;
Offerings are laid
Upon bare earth,
At ve and at harrow.
We find ourselves,
Hammer-thrown
And hallowed.
This is the first and last;
The last and first.
Freyr climbs
To Alfheim-height;
Freyr climbs
Beneath the earth.
Hail the Lord of
Light and Shadow;
Hail the Lord of
Alf and Harrow!
This is the first and last;
The last and first.

It all
Begins
Again....

Free Concordance
available for download at
michelleiacona.com
and
Facebook.com/Iaconagraphy.

Press michelleiacona.com

Iaconagraphy Press is an independent publisher of Pagan and Spiritual non-fiction books, as well as fiction works which reflect those themes. While our focus is primarily on Norse Traditional and Welsh-inspired Paths, we pride ourselves on our authors' ability to surprise the reader with what they find discussed upon the pages of our books. We are dedicated to producing books which promote social justice and empathy, inspiring our readers to "think outside the box" and challenge the spiritual status quo. We strive to produce books which are as visually appealing, as they are thought-provoking: books which you would be as proud to put on display, as you would be to read.

Please visit our website at www.michelleiacona.com to learn more about our upcoming books and for free downloads, and be sure to follow us on Facebook at Iaconagraphy!

The Wheel of Ice and Fire

Working the Wheel as a Norse Witch

by Connla Freyjason

The third book in Connla Freyjason's **Norse Witch Series**, **The Wheel of Ice and Fire** builds upon the foundations of practice set forth in *Norse Witch: Reclaiming the Heidhrinn Heart* and *Blessings of Fire and Ice: A Norse Witch Devotional* to provide a framework for a *living*, *breathing* practice with the Norse Gods and Goddesses. Each month, Connla Freyjason invites the reader to explore animal and stone correspondences, visits to various locations in the Nine Worlds, recipes, rituals, and even holidays, all set against a backdrop of vignettes of daily life in the Old Norse World.

Coming: December 2018 from Iaconagraphy Press

Faith Food Family
Hearthmaking, Hygge, & Heirloom Recipes
for the Modern Kitchen Witch

by Suzanne Hersey

The long-awaited first book from Kitchen Witch Suzanne Hersey, **Faith Food Family** brings ancient traditions of Hearthmaking and Hygge into the modern world, with all of the sass and spice her followers have come to know and love! A host of multi-cultural heirloom recipes are sure to tickle the tastebuds as well as the hearts in your home. There's a bit of witch in all of us: come explore *your* magick!

Coming: October 2018 from Iaconagraphy Press